D1247173

HOW TO BUY PICTURES

Jasper Johns: *False Start I* (Field 10). 1962. Lithograph printed in colours, 44·8 × 34·9 cm.

CHRISTIE'S COLLECTORS GUIDES

HOW TO BUY PICTURES

Practical advice on all aspects
of the art market

HUON MALLALIEU

PRENTICE-HALL, INC., Englewood Cliffs, New Jersey 07632

For Fenella

The views expressed in this Christie's Collectors Guide are those of the author. They do not necessarily reflect the views of Christie, Manson & Woods Ltd.

Acknowledgements

I first began to haunt antique shops and junk-shops at the age of about 10, and for the last fifteen years I have worked in and around the art world. It would take a prodigious memory and another whole book to thank everyone who has contributed to this one in one way or another. Many friends and mentors must therefore be content with only a general 'thank you'. For immediate advice and assistance I am particularly grateful to John Baskett, Stephen Somerville, Robin Garton and Gordon Cooke, to the restorers Richard Knight and Gilli Ardizzone, and to William Mostyn-Owen and Mark Wrey of Christie's. The advice of Jerry Patterson, both specifically on the American market and in general, has been invaluable, and Charles Chrestien's photographs are admirable as always. Thanks, too, to all at Phaidon.

HLM 1984

Library of Congress Cataloguing in Publication Data

Mallalieu, Huon.
    How to buy pictures.
    Includes bibliography and index.
    1.   Art—Collectors and collecting.
    I.   Title.
ISBN 0–13–396599–6

First published in the United States of America 1984
by Prentice-Hall, Inc., Englewood Cliffs, New Jersey 07632

Typeset by Keyspools Ltd, Bridge Street, Golborne, Lancs.

Printed and bound in England by Butler & Tanner Limited, Frome, Somerset

Contents

1. Introduction

It is very difficult to set practical limits to a book such as this. Almost every culture and period in the history of mankind has produced some sort of pictorial art, and the few exceptions have usually expressed themselves in sculpture and carving. It will not be possible to cover every area of picture collecting in detail here, but I hope that the general principles of how to look can be applied to many more categories and interests than can be discussed individually.

In essence this book will try to deal with every image that is painted or drawn by hand, or printed in ink. It will not concern itself with photographs or photographic reproductions, nor will it touch on near relatives such as needlework samplers and sand pictures. It is written from a broadly western standpoint, and so, even within this wide territory, it will not presume to expertise in such specialist fields as Indian and Persian miniatures, Haitian primitives, icons or Oriental prints and watercolours. However, the mechanics of buying such things are much the same as for an Old Master print or an Impressionist pastel, and the intention of this book is to provide an introduction to the workings of the art market, rather than a guide to the goods on offer.

Many people, and I am certainly one of them, are never entirely happy to live with bare walls, and most of us from time to time have anything from a few pounds to a few thousand pounds to spend on covering them. The great masterpieces which we might hope to own in an ideal world need not concern us overmuch, although, just occasionally, given bad luck and management on the one side and good luck and hard work on the other, a masterwork may in fact still be found in this price range.

Another factor which has to be considered by most people is the amount of space available. Probably one of the reasons for the renewed popularity of watercolours and prints over the last few decades is that their scale and proportions so often accord with many modern houses and rooms which might be overawed by larger and more assertive oil paintings. Many contemporary artists work on a large scale, and this should be considered when choosing a field. Without a good deal of space it is not always satisfactory to mix oil paintings with watercolours, prints and drawings. In general I prefer to segregate them in different rooms, or

David Hockney: *Sun*, from the Weather Series. 1973. Lithograph, image and paper size 95 × 78 cm.

sun

75/98   david hockney 73

at least on different walls, although as always there are exceptions which can live very happily together.

Given such inevitable limitations there is only one fundamental rule for the collector of pictures: buy what you like, and not what other people tell you you should like.

As I write about the art market, the uncongenial business of house-buying is constantly forcing itself upon my attention. In one way this is a good thing, since I notice more and more parallels between the two activities. The over-optimistic cataloguing, with its sometimes misleading jargon, is often much the same; similar hidden expenses can trap the unwary; condition in each case can only be assessed by you and can never be taken on trust; no two houses or pictures are ever quite the same. Most strikingly, with both pictures and the house in which to hang them, your most satisfactory acquisition in the long run will often be something that you fell in love with but could only afford with difficulty.

However, while the house-buyer must consider the investment potential of his purchase before buying it, the picture collector should never buy for investment, since all too often this means that he will buy badly and without love. On the other hand the collection or single painting that is bought for its quality and with love will often turn out to be an excellent investment also.

Any business activity has its rules and habits, and the art world is no exception. With or without reason many people regard picture dealers as plausible and seedy swindlers and auctioneers as supercilious and well-dressed parasites. Naturally enough some few of them do live down to expectation. For the most part, though, they are more or less knowledge-able professionals, and it is to their professional advantage to help the buyer as much as they can. The quick shearing of the innocent may well have its attractions, but much more so the fostering of an enthusiastic and

George Wright: *The Kill* (one of a pair). Oil, 19 × 29·1 cm.

Sporting paintings are not always judged by art alone. Wright, for instance, was no great artist, but his subject matter makes him sought after and comparatively expensive. This painting sold for £2,800 at auction in 1978.

Samuel Atkins: *Cutters by a Quay in Dover Harbour*. Signed and dated 1805. Watercolour, 27·9 × 39 cm.

For many collectors of marine paintings and watercolours too subject is more important than art, and accuracy is what is demanded. Luckily many marine painters have been excellent artists as well as technicians, although they are rarely stylistic innovators.

increasingly educated client who will return again and again over the years.

There are as many reasons for buying pictures as there are picture buyers, and people may begin for any one of them. There are those who become collectors almost by mistake. They buy one thing to fill a space or to complete a decorative scheme, and then gradually want another and another. They may be intrigued by a particular artist and acquire more and more of his work. Their first interest may be a specific place, a country, town or even a building, and from this they come to love the paintings and painters who represent it. Many, notably doctors, dentists and scientists, seek out illustrations of the history of their professions. I know an aristocrat who must have every view of the long-sold family seat, and a tennis player who is avid for every depiction of the game from *jeu de paume* to pharistiké and Wimbledon.

Every few decades an eighteenth-century pastel of one John Walter appears on the London market. The current editor of *The Times* gets excited about it and sends someone – usually the sale room correspondent – to investigate. So far they have been lucky and have found out in time that, although a namesake, this Mr Walter was only a remote relative of the founder of 'The Thunderer' and does not deserve an honoured place in the boardroom.

Mixed motives do not necessarily mean the buying of bad art. Late nineteenth-century sophisticates might have mocked the new rich British industrialists who bought safe landscapes and sugary genre subjects, and in the same way it has long been customary for some Europeans to look down on the American magnates who bought very expensive ancestry from the great dealer Joseph Duveen in the first part of this century. However, many of these 'barbarians' have left their descendants or their Foundations with some very fine paintings. A slightly more subtle version of this innocent snobbery is shown by the racehorse owner or trainer who collects portraits of the great sires and dams of the past. It is establishing a claim to ancestral respectability – even if at one remove – to be able to point out of the window and say: '. . . and there is his great-great grandson'. This little pleasure, too, has been the foundation of some great collections.

For some of us the great collectors of the past are almost as fascinating as the works of art that they collected. A painting is valuable to us not only because of its inherent beauty, but also because it once belonged to someone whom we admire. I myself am always tempted by drawings and paintings actually executed by great collectors and patrons, many of whom were able amateur practitioners; it is a form of homage to men and women who did not always receive due gratitude from their protégés, or understanding from their relatives.

An ironic illustration of this last occurred a few years ago, when the cousins of Lord Brooke publicly objected to his selling of the family collections at Warwick Castle. When the collection was formed by the second Earl of Warwick in the eighteenth century, his relations had taken out court orders to prevent him from setting foot in the castle and frittering the family fortunes away on art and artists. Thus does one generation's folly become another's heritage.

Thomas Girtin: *The Village of Jedburgh, Roxburgh*. 1800. Watercolour, 30·2 × 52·1 cm.

This is obviously right out of our price range, but it is well worth illustrating as a splendid example of its type, school and date.

Daniel Gardner: *Portrait of Rebecca, Lady Rushout (Baroness Northwick) and her Three Elder Children, Anne, Harriet and John (later 2nd Lord Northwick)*. 1777 (?). Pastel and bodycolour, oval, on paper laid on canvas, 66·4 × 83·8 cm.

Eighteenth-century pastels are easily damaged and impossible to repair. From this point of view Gardner is worth singling out, since his characteristic mixture of pastel and paint was more robust.

From the purely mercenary point of view, as we shall see at a later point, a good 'provenance' – the fact that a painting has been in a good collection in the past – can increase its monetary value in the future. It can also be reassuring to know that we are not alone in considering something beautiful and that the connoisseurs of the past agreed with us.

Most people begin by buying only one thing, or at any rate just a few examples. A few prefer to acquire a ready-made collection in one go. The latter course naturally requires greater resources, and it also cuts out much of the excitement of the pursuit, which is one of the greatest pleasures of collecting. It is a little like getting an interior-decorator to provide you with a pleasant place to live. On the other hand even such an off-the-peg collection need not be regarded as static and fixed for all time, and it can be an admirable and easy way to begin. In fact, unless it has a particular homogeneity, or aims to be definitive in its field, a collection is likely to be ever changing.

It is often the case that as our taste, or pocket, improves, early acquisitions no longer satisfy. However, in the nature of things prices will probably have risen in the interim, and ideally the sale of such items should fund the buying of better examples. Thus, in theory, a collection (like a good wine-cellar) can become virtually self-supporting through the process known as 'trading up'. In reality, improved taste, as in any other sphere, is likely to lead to still greater expenditure. Obviously, too, this method of proceeding will not appeal to those who wanted only one particular thing in the first place, or who have sentimental reasons for holding onto their early purchases.

Successful trading up takes us back to the idea of investment, at least in practice if not in original intention. Picture-buying purely to make money should be left to the well-financed and experienced professionals; beginners need only be aware that it is done. The re-establishment of a market for an overlooked artist or school, for instance, is a long, complicated and sometimes costly exercise. To begin with you must collect as many good quality works as possible, and be prepared to sit on your investment. You must then establish a sale-room track-record at the sort of levels you wish. Then an exhibition must be mounted and publicized. All too often the private speculator lacks the time, the resources and the knowledge to undertake such an enterprise.

Similarly with single examples: the painting that appears to the amateur to be under-priced may in fact be no such thing. It is possibly merely bad – even though it may be by an artist who can be very good on other occasions – and it will never rise in price in relative market terms. In recent years it has also become more difficult for the amateur to hear about potential rises in the market until they are well under way. Since the 1950s almost every type of painting, school and artist has found favour, and if a dealer has managed to corner the market in an obscure but profitable talent, he is unlikely to let the world know about it until he is ready to exploit it to the full.

Timing is of the utmost importance in the art market, and the lure of the possible quick return must often be resisted. Many people have come sadly unstuck by assuming that paintings can be bought and re-sold at auction as quickly and easily as stocks and shares. However, when a well-known painting has been through a sale, the market is rightly suspicious if it re-appears too soon. Conventional wisdom says that about ten years should intervene, although, as always, there are many exceptions. In short, investment for the dealer is a matter of long and careful planning. For the collector it should be fortuitous, an added bonus to his pleasure.

A little while ago I mentioned that it is occasionally possible to buy a great masterpiece within the limits that we are discussing. It is possible, but it is not something that you should expect to happen. The most celebrated case in recent years concerned *Psyche Showing her Sisters her Gifts from Cupid* by Jean Honoré Fragonard (1732–1806), which now

Sir Joseph Duveen (1869–1939), later Lord Duveen, dominated the international art market in the first half of the twentieth century, selling European paintings to American millionaires at the highest possible prices. He created a fashion, among other things, for eighteenth-century British portraits, and their prices have probably never been higher in real terms than in the twenties and early thirties.

Albert Anker: *Portrait of Frau Marie Zimmermann* (née Schönauer), half length. Commissioned 1892. Signed, canvas laid down on board, 54·6 × 41·2 cm.

One portrait such as this can add distinction to a collection. Several, unless of your own family, would weigh it down.

(*Below*) Thomas Gainsborough: *Blue Boy* (Jonathan Buttall). Exhibited 1770. Canvas, 177·8 × 122 cm. San Marino, California, Henry E. Huntington Library and Art Gallery.

One of the greatest American acquisitions during the boom in English portraits inspired by Duveen.

hangs in honour in the National Gallery in London. Until 1977 it was an almost unnoticed wall-filler in the Rosebery-Rothschild Collection at Mentmore Towers in Buckinghamshire. At the celebrated sale in May of that year it was catalogued as *The Toilet of Venus* by the artist Charles-André, known as Carle, van Loo (1705–65), who was a good but not overly distinguished man of the mid-eighteenth century. The auctioneers had put a pre-sale estimate of from £8,000 to £12,000 on it, and on the day of sale it reached £8,000. Nothing untoward in that, but the buyer was the dealer David Carritt, which may have given sensitive cataloguers a momentary frisson of unease, since his nose for a dramatic discovery was well proven. It did not fail him on this occasion, and shortly afterwards he was able to announce the sale to the National Gallery of the supposedly

lost student picture which Fragonard had painted for the École des Élèves Protégés in 1753. The sum was not disclosed, but informed guesses of around £400,000 were denied by neither party to the deal.

The career of David Carritt, who sadly died at a comparatively early age a few years later, should be studied by any would-be collector, and certainly by anyone with an ambition to become a picture dealer. The casual elegance with which he would unveil a discovery said much for his theatrical flair, but it made what had often been detective work of the most painstaking order seem mere good luck. He adopted the dictum of Sherlock Holmes: 'when you have eliminated the impossible, whatever remains, *however improbable*, must be the truth', and put it to gentler use than the unmasking of Moriarty. Cold logic, allied to a well-trained and particularly sensitive eye, led him to great paintings that others had presumed long destroyed – for example the four paintings by Canaletto (1720–80) which were rolled up in a Dublin potting-shed, and were unknown even to the owner of the house.

Jean Honoré Fragonard: *Psyche Showing her Sisters her Gifts from Cupid*. 1753. Oil, 19·5 × 22·8 cm. London, National Gallery.

(*Opposite*) Albert Goodwin: *St. Mark's, Venice: The West Doors and the Piazzetta*. Signed and dated 91. Pencil and watercolour, 17·1 × 24·8 cm.

Goodwin is now accepted as a good and expensive painter, but his market was created by the hard work of two dealers, one in the late sixties, the other in the early eighties.

John Frederick Lewis:
Highland Hospitality.
Exhibited 1832.
Watercolour heightened
with white,
54·9 × 74·9 cm. The
importance of subject in
making price must not be
forgotten. Lewis was a
fine artist, whether in
Scotland, on the
Continent, or in the
Middle East, but
Orientalist works are
much the most expensive.
The quality of this
Scottish scene, which
includes portraits of his
fellow artists George
Cattermole and William
Evans, is similar to the
Egyptian and Tyrolean
subjects illustrated on
pages 23 and 24, but the
price hierarchy would be:
Egypt, Scotland, the
Continent.

On occasions good luck did play a part and saved a long and dusty search, as when Carritt located a ceiling-painting by Giovanni Battista Tiepolo (1696–1770) that had been assumed lost since about 1922. At that time it had adorned the London house of the collector Bischoffsheim, and it was last recorded on the death of his widow, when the house was sold to the Egyptian government as its embassy. Carritt could find no record of a sale, so he visited the embassy to see whether any documents relating to the painting survived there. Once inside he looked up and there was Tiepolo's *Allegory of Venus Entrusting Eros to Chronos* exactly where it had always been. One wonders how many experts and connoisseurs who should have recognized it, or at least its quality, had attended receptions and parties at the embassy over the years. The Tiepolo, too, is now in the London National Gallery.

In the case of the Mentmore painting the documentary evidence was there for anyone who cared to look and knew where to begin. Carritt's eye told him that it was too good to be by the second rank van Loo, and he knew that the artist had never painted the subject or one that could be mistaken for it. But then van Loo had been Fragonard's first teacher. A short trawl through the standard works came up with a description of the painting under its correct title. If a private collector of limited means had done his homework he would have come up against Carritt, whose resources would have been the greater, but the remarkable thing is that there would have been no opposition from other dealers or from museum curators, and the whole of the international art world had viewed and been present at the sale.

That this sort of thing can still happen, if only very occasionally, is one of the great attractions of the art world. Most of the time, however, most of us will be looking for humbler works, and the first thing to decide is what we really want from the vast numbers of examples of different schools and

(*Right*) Giovanni Battista Tiepolo: *An Allegory of Venus Entrusting Eros to Chronos* (also known as *An Allegory of Venus with Time*). *c.*1758. Oil, 115 × 75 cm. London, National Gallery.

(*Below*) The 'rediscovered' painting leaves home.

types on offer. Thereafter we must ensure that we are getting the best available at the best possible price.

Obviously anyone can look at a picture just as anyone can listen to a piece of music, but as with listening there are degrees of looking, and the better trained and exercised the ear or eye, the greater the pleasure to be derived from its function. In *The Light that Failed* Kipling describes a group of soldiers criticizing a battle picture in the window of a gallery. They discuss it from a keenly professional point of view, admiring the accurate detailing of equipment and the truth of the action. They are carried into the story and carry it forward to what must happen next. Undoubtedly these soldiers derived pleasure from the painting, but it was a limited one, such as could have given by a good photograph, and they showed no interest in the tricks of composition and foreshortening, the brushwork and the handling of paint by which it had been produced.

It is perhaps worth while cribbing a technique from the music critic Eric Blom, who distinguishes three degrees of aural appreciation. As visual equivalents we might suggest looking, viewing and seeing. Looking is the most superficial. It is the rather unfocused pleasure gained from the awareness of an agreeable arrangement of colours, or from the suggestion of a story or train of thought. Kipling's troopers were looking, since their interest was in the incident depicted rather than in the work of art as a

Orlando Norie: *Royal Horse Artillery: a Troop Advancing at a Gallop*. Signed. Watercolour and bodycolour, 32·4 × 49·5 cm.

One of the nineteenth-century painters who made a career of portraying regiments with the emphasis on accuracy rather than artistry.

Sir David Young Cameron: *Ben Ledi*.
1911. Etching, 37·7 x 30·2 cm.

One of the great works of the British etching revival in the first part of the twentieth century.

whole, of which the subject was only one ingredient.

Viewing is very much more specific. It is the careful examination and analysis of the surface accidents and mechanics – condition, technique, subject matter and style in so far as it tells us about period and authorship – together with such background incidentals as provenance, mounting and framing. Aesthetic pleasure may certainly be a part of it, but on the whole viewing is a cool and forensic activity.

In seeing, we are fully aware of all the technical factors learnt from viewing. We know how and why it was done, but our thoughts and emotions are caught and steered in just the way intended by the artist. We are pulled out of ourselves and for a moment are one in experience with everyone else who has seen that picture, and with the artist himself. In music this last stage has been described as listening, as opposed to hearing or overhearing, but the parallels are not exact. Naturally, too, as with music, the three degrees may overlap or flow into each other.

This seeming digression has not in fact been one, for just as the music-lover will develop his ear, or the wine expert his palate, by practice, so the connoisseur of pictures must stretch the capacity of his eye by constant exercise. He must study the best available on all possible occasions, and he must also analyse the worst whenever he comes across it, which will probably be still more frequently.

All too often people either laugh at an expertise that they do not themselves possess, or react to it as if it were some kind of magic. It is particularly difficult and risible to try to translate the operations of one sense into the language of another, as both wine experts and the writers of erotic prose so often discover. This danger is very present when one tries to describe an 'eye' or a 'feel' for the beautiful, but it must be risked.

The operation of a trained eye is automatic and so fast as to be virtually instinctive. This is why many a good expert, when questioned about his reasoning after a snap decision, will sound evasive and unconvincing. In the same way a computer that can usually tell you 'what', often has difficulty with 'why?' The mind must sift through perhaps thousands of previous visual experiences, collating painting techniques, composition, subject matter, condition, provenance and comparable examples. The first reaction of someone with a good eye is usually the right one, and cooler, more logical second thoughts can very often mislead.

It has been convincingly claimed that it is possible for a blind person to develop the sense of touch to such a pitch of sensitivity as to be able to distinguish colours through the fingertips. This comes as no surprise to anyone who is accustomed to handling bronzes, pottery, porcelain or fine woods. However, it is not generally recognized that the quality of almost any work of art – including paintings – can be sensed through the hands. There is quite a noticeable tingle, or an equally palpable feeling of deadness. Once again, with experience, the first impression is right more often than not.

This sort of instinctive skill is invaluable, but as far as possible it must always be backed up by hard facts. The self-deluded abound in the art world as much as, if not more than, elsewhere in life. For some reason Goya seems to have crazed more than most, but it can happen with the most

A. J. Moor: *Still Life*. Undated. Oil, 74·3 × 60·3 cm.

apparently sane of collectors and the most unassuming of artists and paintings. One man in recent years is reputed to have spent about half a million pounds in a forlorn effort to prove that a trivial drawing came from a particular master's hand. Even if, by a miracle, he was right, such a doodle could only be worth some £200 as a curiosity. Another fanatic swears that he can see so many devious miniature signatures per square inch on his dreary painting. Of course, given sufficient magnification you

William Duffield: *Still Life*. Oil,
90 × 71 cm.

can read any significance you wish into the chance markings of a paint surface, but no artist with a living to earn could have wasted his time with such childishness. This sort of thing is on a level with the secrets of the Pyramids and the Lost Tribes of Israel, and if you ever notice any symptoms of it in yourself, forget about pictures and go for a long winter cruise or a bout of bricklaying.

A true eye must then be a clear one, and in theory the picture buyer's head should also be level and his heart steady. Decide what you want and whether you intend to buy just one thing or start a collection. Do your sums and go out and get it. It seems simple enough, but luckily things very rarely work out like that. The person who wants a specific picture will find himself amassing a collection, and if you know that you cannot afford a particular object, you will almost always return home with it and its still more expensive stable-mate under your arm.

There is no point in advising you as to what type of picture you should collect. If you are fated to be a true collector, the type, school, medium or whatever, will choose you, despite what anyone else may say. You may well have already bought your first example or examples. It is important, if you are new to it and suspect that the addiction has taken hold, that you should buy no more for a good while.

Anyone who knows that he is going to buy more than one or two pictures, and treats it as more than an exercise in decoration, should be prepared to do a little homework. After all, you would if it was a case of choosing a new washing-machine, a doctor, a solicitor, a wife, or a husband. Why should the arts, which can be just as expensive, be treated more carelessly? First read a good general history of your subject – a few suggestions for essential reading in some of the fields are given in the bibliography – and then go out and look.

Ideally, before you buy anything else you should spend six months or so going to the viewing days for auctions and to all relevant exhibitions. You should studiously ignore all auctioneers' pre-sale estimates and all dealers' price lists until you have viewed everything very thoroughly and marked up your own catalogue. You should write in not only your own guesses at to price, but also all that you can tell about condition and subject, and everything that will help you to remember what you saw months or even years later. One of the most important components of a good eye is a well-trained visual memory. It will not be enough to think that you have seen something of the sort before. You must know that it really was comparable, or in what respects it differed, and exactly when and where you saw it. This may save you from making expensive mistakes in the future.

Having made your notes and estimates you should then look at the price list if you are at an exhibition, or try to attend the sale – still without buying. If you cannot attend a sale you can telephone the auctioneers later for the prices of the lots that particularly interested you, or you can subscribe for the complete price lists. The main advantage of being present is that you can get the feel of the market and some knowledge of procedure. Was the bidding competitive or sluggish? Which dealers were most interested in which lots and artists? Why? Could you tell when a lot failed to sell and was bought in? Did it appear that a boom in any particular artist's work was under way, or that another might be going out of fashion? Did you notice (and note) significant variations in price which seemed unjustifed by quality? For instance, a Greek or Eastern subject by an artist may have made more than a better executed view of Hastings by the same man. If a good-looking picture made significantly less than you expected, had you gathered that it had already been over-exposed, that is

John Frederick Lewis: *Indoor Gossip, Cairo*. 1873. Oil, 30·4 × 20·2 cm. Manchester, Whitworth Art Gallery.

to say offered to the main dealers or included in a recent sale?

A further advantage of attending in person is that you will feel more at ease when the time comes to make your first bid. However, the conventions of bidding and sale-room practice will be discussed later and need not detain us here.

Because of the dictates of business or the restrictions imposed by place of residence many people, of course, will be unable to view the best sales in a concentrated manner, but they can at least subscribe to the catalogues and study the prices. There is and can be no substitute for looking for yourself, but this will be a small and worthwhile start. At the same time you must haunt whatever art galleries and museums there may be in your area, and see if you can gain entry to any of the better private collections that you know of.

I have already stated that you must never think that something is good merely because other people say that it is. You must make up your own mind. Andrew Wyld, a leading London dealer in drawings and water-

John Frederick Lewis: *Peasant and Monk at a Roadside Shrine in the Tyrol*. Signed and dated 1829. Watercolour heightened with white, 48·6 × 62 cm.

colours, goes still further. According to him the fundamental law for any buyer of pictures, whether dealer or collector, is never to believe anything that anyone says unless they can offer the most solid supporting evidence. Just because something hangs imposingly in a museum, or is fulsomely catalogued by an auctioneer, it does not always follow that it is what it is claimed to be: dealers, auctioneers, museum curators and the most eminent experts can all make mistakes, thank heavens. If everyone always knew exactly what everything was and how much it was worth there would be no discoveries and ultimately no trade. The collector would also lose a great deal of fun and satisfaction.

The corollary, of course, is that you must never assume that you know better than everyone else without equally clear-eyed testing. What seems to you to be the most wonderful bargain may very easily turn out to be quite the opposite.

If you do make such a mistake, and almost everybody will, you should keep it constantly by you as a reminder. I still have my first, a 'Romney' portrait of Lady Hamilton. In my innocent youth I believed the inscription on the back and spent all my pocket-money on a very undistinguished Victorian copy. If after a while you find that your gallery of reminders outnumbers your collection of bargains, then perhaps you should look elsewhere for a hobby!

2. Sources of Advice and Information

The first person to turn to for advice when you are offered a picture is yourself. If you like it so much that questions of exact authorship, subject, price, condition and provenance are irrelevant, then no more need be said; go ahead and buy it. If not, you owe it to yourself to find out as much as possible before parting with your money, and a great deal of the basic research is a matter of simple common sense.

This chapter will have little in it for the buyers of contemporary works, where the decision is governed solely by what you, or your bank manager, think you can afford. As with any other modern product which may or may not increase in value in the future, the immediate market is set by the creator, or his agent if he has one. The only criticism and commentary is likely to be in magazines and newspapers. With older works there are many other factors to consider, and even if you have only a short time in which to make up your mind, there are a number of steps which you can take to ensure satisfaction, or at least to make the decision easier.

Unfortunately time is often at a premium. There may be only a day, or even a few hours, between a view and a sale, or there may be likely competition at a dealer's exhibition. In such cases one must concentrate only on the basic essentials: is it in fact what it is supposed to be, or could it perhaps be something better? Is it worth the asking price, or how much is it safe to bid at auction? If you can satisfy yourself as to these points, further researches may be carried out at leisure.

While one should not always disclose the strength of one's interest or the extent of one's knowledge, it is all too easy to make the mistake of treating every vendor, whether private individual, dealer or auctioneer, as an adversary. Generally, in fact, it is in their interest to see that you are fairly treated and well suited. Whether you buy or not on the first occasion, a good dealer will want your custom for the future. The first step, then, is to glean all the information possible from the catalogue if there is one, and then to see whether the seller has any further comments or tips to add. It is often useful to know something of the recent history of a picture, and with this in mind you should always look at the back, even if it is in an obviously new frame. On an old back-board or canvas you will

The reverse side of Lucio Fontana's *Concetto Spaziale – Attesa* (see page 127). Always look at the back of a painting. Here we have exhibition stamps and labels as well as a Christie's chalk and stencil stock number.

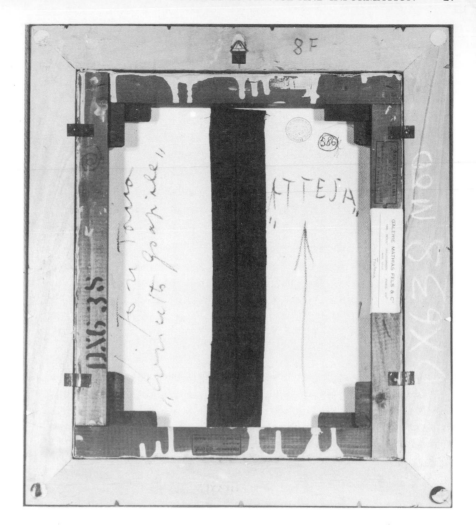

very often find information which will confirm or demolish an attribution, or at least help you to form your own theory. Even if the picture has been reframed recently a conscientious dealer or owner should have transferred any relevant information from the old frame to the new, and noted any inscriptions on the reverse which may have been covered up.

A particularly useful discovery on a back-board or a stretcher is a stencilled combination of letters and numbers such as 567 VH. All framed pictures handled by Christie's are marked in this way, and there are often also chalked sale dates and lot numbers. If you ring up or call to make an enquiry, the number will be looked up for you and such information as is available will be passed on to you; but it is as well to give as full a description as possible, since such stock numbers refer to properties rather than to individual items, and so may appear on several different paintings. On really old properties the firm will reveal the name of the vendor as well as the details of the sale if they were recorded, but confidentiality is observed on vendors' names, unless they are included in the catalogue, for fifty years. If the chalk marks include no sale date, but rather a capital 'N', beware, since this means that it was not considered to be of sufficient value to be worth offering. Equally, if there are several dates covering a short period, be cautious. The picture may have failed to sell on one or more occasions.

Unfortunately Christie's are the only firm to use a permanent stock-marking system in this way, and in the early 1970s they gave up the use of natural chalk, which tended to scratch the surface; so later chalked sale and lot numbers may have rubbed off. Sotheby's numbers — such as 725074/2, indicating two items in the property — are sometimes chalked on, and sometimes written on sticky labels of about one inch in length. These last may have left a mark. Phillips often use blue chalk. In the same way, a dealer or frame-maker may have stamped his label with a stock number, and if the firm and its records are still in existence these too can be checked.

The major auction houses in the U.S. and a good many of the smaller ones have numbered their sales from opening. Parke-Bernet Galleries, for instance, held sale number one in January 1938. After merging with Sotheby's in 1964, the same numbering system was continued. In theory, each lot has carried a sticker or tag giving sale and lot numbers; in practice, the sale number has often been omitted, and the lot number is of little use without the sale or date. Nevertheless, a good many sale stickers are still found on stretchers or print mounts and are invaluable in tracing provenance. In addition, sale and lot numbers, some dating to the nineteenth century, are found chalked or pencilled on the back of paintings or drawings.

Exhibition labels will often give details about the artist and about the picture itself. If the gallery concerned was of even moderate respectability, these can be checked against the original catalogue entry without great difficulty. In Britain those galleries which have survived have usually kept good records, and the files of those that have not have often found their way to the Victoria and Albert Museum, the British Library or the local art gallery. Some dealers will also put a stock number on their labels: numbers placed by Agnew's, one of the most prominent picture dealers in London, for instance, can be checked back for over a hundred years.

Such major art libraries are obvious hunting-grounds for anyone researching a picture, but there are others which are also of great value, but may escape notice. That at the Royal Academy is open to the public every weekday afternoon. One of its many attractions is a run of exhibition catalogues which has been interleaved with reviews, illustrations and comments. A few hundred yards away, in St. James's Square, is the London Library, which is, in a modest way, one of the glories of the capital. It is open to members only, but is well worth its subscription, since the picture researcher needs very much more than the ordinary specialized art reference section. One never knows what byways will have to be explored, and as at the London Library virtually everything is on open shelves, it is a perfect place for the rambler who needs to be able to move from place to place following hints and clues without endless waiting and form-filling.

The Londoner, too, is lucky in the art reference section of the

A porter at Christie's applying the stencilled stock number.

Westminster Public Library, which has many of the basic works; the library is in St. Martin's Street, between Leicester Square and the back of the National Gallery.

The National Gallery itself, the National Portrait Gallery, the National Maritime Museum at Greenwich, the Imperial War Museum, the National Army Museum, the India Office Library and many others all have a part to play, and there are specialized organizations and groups, from the Royal Institute of British Architects to the Royal Zoological Society, which may be able to solve problems of subject or even attribution.

The search for an attribution will, and should, often lead to the Witt Library, which is part of the Courtauld Institute at 20 Portman Square, London W.1. This was founded and built up by Sir Robert Witt, a most notable connoisseur, and now contains over a million and a quarter photographs of European paintings and drawings from the Renaissance to the present day. Not only will you be able to compare the picture that

Members of Christie's picture department examining an oil painting.

interests you with others by the same artist or school, or with other versions of the subject, but, if you are lucky, you may even find the picture itself, photographed at an earlier stage in its career. This may also be a short cut to finding out about previous sales and history, since illustrations from auction and exhibition catalogues are kept here, as well as specially commissioned photographs and examples from museums and private collections.

When, in time, you have collected important items yourself, it is no bad thing to lodge photographs at the Witt. Not only will they be of benefit to scholars, but, should the worst befall, they will be an aid to the police or your insurance company.

Most of the larger museums in the U.S. maintain extensive art reference libraries that are generally open to the public for research. Especially notable are those at the Frick Musuem and the Metropolitan Museum in New York City, the Art Institute of Chicago, and the Cleveland Museum of Art. Libraries such as the New York Public Library and the Library of Congress, both open without charge to anyone, have important art research facilities.

University libraries in the U.S., where art history is one of the most important undergraduate fields, have large collections. Unless one is a student at the university, these generally impose a small fee for research. The libraries at Columbia University, New York City, and Harvard

The Reading Room of the British Library.

The London Library.

University, Cambridge, Mass., are among the largest and best organized, but smaller universities across the country maintain art reference libraries that can be a quickly accessible resource for the collector doing research.

By this point you will have realized that the business of research can be both time-consuming and frustrating, and you might well feel that it would be better to call in a professional picture researcher. This is a most useful service for those who cannot afford to traipse round collections and libraries themselves, and it is also used by a number of leading dealers in the preparation of exhibition catalogues.

Information as to reasonable prices must come largely from personal observation. There are, of course, various price guides giving auction results for each year, and the information accumulated by the Art Sales Index organization of Pond House, Weybridge, Surrey, is now available as a computer service. Several computer services supplying the prices of paintings have been established in the U.S., among them Artscan and Tele-appraisal, both in New York City. These supply either verbal information or a print-out of artists' prices upon payment of a fee. Users must always remember, though, that when dealing with pictures a recorded price is only applicable to one particular object at one particular

The Witt Library (British School) at the Courtauld Institute of Art, London.

moment. Only the widest generalizations can be drawn from it. Price guides are also limited in that they can only accept the information given in an auctioneer's catalogue at face value, and if this is wrong the true facts will either be distorted or not given at all. In fact, such guides are primarily of use to the experienced professional, as a convenient *aide-mémoire*, rather than to the collector making occasional forays into the market.

One of the most sensible things that a collector can do in the early stages is to find a reputable dealer on whose advice he can rely, and whom he can use where necessary as a buying agent either at sales or from other galleries. A representative of an auction house will of course give you good advice, but since his prime duty is to sell the goods for his client, he can only act within certain circumscribed limits. A good dealer should have a much more extensive overview of the market than is usually available to a single auctioneer or private buyer. A dealer, for instance, might be able to tell you to hold back from a painting in a London sale because a better example will shortly be appearing in the country, where it might well be less expensive. Even if an auctioneer happened to know this, it would be against his interests and those of his vendor to pass on the information.

If you are contemplating buying a painting that is in less than perfect condition, or one that you fear may have been tampered with, then ask a professional restorer to view it with you. Most will do this free of charge, providing that you do not waste their time too often, on the understanding that they will get the job if you are successful. This will help you to decide what sort of bid is worth while, and save you from unexpected expenses afterwards. Once again, this sort of exact information is unlikely to be available from the auction house experts, since restoration and its costs very rarely come within the scope of their job. On the other hand, both they and the dealers will be able to advise you on other after-sale costs, such as insurance and shipping. If, at a later stage, you become a seller, the major British auction houses will also be able to advise you on any tax problems, but those in America will refer you to a specialist accountant or tax lawyer.

Because of the dual nature of the pursuit, at the same time so wide-ranging and yet subject to the infinite vagaries of personal inclination, there are no societies or groups dedicated solely to the collection of paintings. However, there are many bodies whose activities impinge upon it, and which may prove invaluable to the collector.

In Britain, perhaps the greatest of these is the National Art-Collections Fund, a private organization which, since its foundation in 1903, has done so much to keep so many national treasures in the country. Apart from its lectures, tours, visits and other activities, it is of particular importance to the collector in that its membership-card gives access to a number of major libraries and museum facilities, including the Victoria and Albert Museum Library and Students' Room, the British Library and the Print Room at the British Museum.

The growth of interest in antiques and the fine arts over the last few decades has been such that the country is now covered by a network of local groups and societies which either take a general interest or are dedicated to a specific subject. To find out which best suits your needs is a fairly simple business, since there is now also a blanket-grouping, the National Association of Decorative and Fine Art Societies, with its headquarters at 38 Ebury Street, London, SW1W 0LU, which can supply lists and details. Other useful groups are the Friends which have formed around almost every cultural institution from the Royal Academy and the Tate Gallery to the smallest local museum.

One of the oldest of this type is the Old Water-Colour Society's Club, which was founded in 1923 and is affiliated to what is now the Royal Society of Painters in Water-Colours based at the Bankside Gallery, 48 Hopton Street, Blackfriars, London SE1 9JH. Even if the collector of English watercolours is unable to gain possession of the early annual volumes published by the Club, since they are now expensive collectors' items in their own right, he should certainly make sure that he has access to a run of them at a library.

Organizations of 'friends', or 'associates', of museums, galleries, libraries, and historical societies are numbered in the hundreds, if not thousands, in the U.S. Annual fees entitle members to the use of reference libraries, lectures, receptions, exhibitions and tours. There are even a few organizations devoted to one artist and his work, such as 'The Friends of Chagall'. Membership as a 'friend' can be an important asset to a tyro collector as he or she can not only learn from the programmes but can meet like-minded collectors and professional art historians, curators and writers.

Membership fees on an annual basis vary from the nominal ($10–25) to the quite expensive ($1,000 or more). Since there are likely to be a number of organizations in even the smaller cities, it is best to shop around or go as a guest to a meeting before deciding which it will be most useful and enjoyable to join.

Until it closed in 1951, the Burlington Fine Arts Club, with premises off Piccadilly, was a gentleman's club, with a membership made up of connoisseurs and collectors. To some extent its aims have been adopted by a commercial organization set up in 1966, the Antique Collectors' Club, of Woodbridge in Suffolk. This is in part a publishing operation, specializing in price guides, dictionaries and reference books for collectors in all fields, including pictures. However, it provides many other services for its members, and now has branches throughout the country which organize lectures, meetings, seminars and sales between collectors. There is also a useful magazine, *Antique Collecting*.

The world of antiques is one in which magazines and journals appear and disappear with bewildering frequency. Their titles, too, are often confusingly similar. Of the major publications in Britain the twin poles might be said to be *The Burlington Magazine* and *The Antiques Trade Gazette*. The *Burlington*, like its grander competitors, finds the majority of its readers abroad, since it is required reading for art historians and museum curators as well as for the most important dealers and collectors. Its concern is with scholarship, and it is the natural forum for the discussion of such matters as the re-attribution of the works of John Constable (1776–1837), or an addition to the *œuvre* of the Master of the Female Half-Lengths.

The *Antiques Trade Gazette*, on the other hand, has little to interest the academic. It is a weekly newspaper dealing with auctions, antiques fairs and exhibitions, and it is read by most dealers and auctioneers in Britain, as well as many abroad. It is usually available by subscription only, but the price is worth it for the comprehensive auction calendar alone. It also has an excellent record in helping to bring about the recovery of stolen goods. If you happen to be in Bond Street, single copies along with most other art and antiques magazines can be obtained from the excellent news-stand at the front door of Sotheby's.

Since the change of direction and style of *The Connoisseur*, *Apollo* stands unchallenged next to the *Burlington* in terms of scholarly prestige. It, too, is aimed at the most important collectors, and a large proportion of its readership is overseas. In between the two poles is the fluctuating population of monthly magazines of which *The Antique Collector* and *The Antique Collector and Dealers' Guide* appear to be the most permanent and useful. Of perennial interest, too, is *Country Life*, which is highly favoured by many dealers as a successful vehicle for advertising and where the Readers' Queries column often brings results.

There is an equally wide range of publications in the U.S. *Artnews*, founded in 1902, is the oldest American art magazine still publishing. It contains both critical and news articles and has a market column. The same organization publishes *The Artnewsletter* every two weeks; it is primarily devoted to the market. *International Art Market* is a monthly covering auctions. *Art & Auctions* is primarily a market report also but does contain some articles on collecting. The magazine *Antiques*, a monthly, is largely devoted to American arts and is the most scholarly of the general magazines. For collectors of American paintings it is indispensable.

There are many monthlies devoted to specific areas of painting, such as *Art Forum* (contemporary art), *Southwestern Art* (Western American painting), *American Art Journal* (nineteenth-century American painting and sculpture) and others.

A serious collector will also keep an eye on the auction reports in the national and local papers. The sale room season now covers most of the year, with a lay-off from the beginning of August to the end of September, and *The Times* and the *Daily Telegraph* both have regular columns. The arts page of *The Financial Times* is worth watching on Saturdays, and other papers carry frequent reports from the sale rooms. Given the space allowed by news editors, these reports can rarely delve deeply into the factors which have produced or influenced prices, but they can provide useful straws in the wind.

Very few newspapers in the U.S. run auction columns – the New York *Times* is an exception – and, in general, to get after-sale reports and commentary it is necessary to subscribe to one of the newsletters or magazines mentioned above. Many newpapers, however, have an antiques or collecting column, especially in the Sunday editions, that can be useful.

The secret of professional life is to know who to ask, and this is as true of collecting as of anything else. There is almost certainly an expert in or a source of information on anything you may need to find out. If you are to be a good collector you must know who and where. If by chance there is no expert, and the subject is worth while, then do the spadework yourself and become the expert to whom everyone else must apply.

Salvador Dali's *Sleep* arriving for auction at Christie's.

3. The Business of Buying

In the second half of the twentieth century auctions and auction houses have come to exercise a fascination over the mind of the public which has sometimes made the uninformed unduly suspicious of dealers. This has been achieved by an adroit use of public relations, and was by no means always the case. Nowadays the auctioneer appears to be unbiased, with no personal interest in the wares which he offers. At the upper end of his trade he goes about his affairs with an opulent confidence which inspires trust, and the publicity which attends his successes often draws in people who would never venture inside a dealer's gallery, however respectable and well established. Bolstered by a couple of centuries of tradition the grand auction house is regarded as an institution, more so than even such a firm of dealers as Spink & Son, which was founded in 1666, the year of the Great Fire of London.

In fact the auctioneer is in something of a dilemma when pursuing clients. On the one hand he must attract vendors by proving that he can get higher prices than anyone else. On the other he must imply to would-be purchasers that it is possible to buy more cheaply at his sales than elsewhere. The more diplomatic rarely make the mistake of putting the two claims to the same client. Bargains certainly attract buyers, but too many of them naturally repel vendors, and without vendors the auctioneer must seek alternative employment.

Some years ago I acted as London agent for a Canadian collector of English watercolours. He would only allow me to buy for him at the major auction houses, even though there were sometimes better or cheaper examples to be had from the dealers. His reasoning was that at the time few Canadians knew or cared much about the subject, and if he ever had to resell the collection at home, the hallowed names of Christie and Sotheby would ensure a respect that no dealer's label, however august in British eyes, could command. He himself loved David Cox and John Sell Cotman well enough, but only the endorsement of a sale-room history and catalogue entry could ensure their acceptance by his countrymen. This attitude was perfectly reasonable at the time, but the English watercolour school is now much better established in the international consciousness, and it is a pity that we had to pass up a number of good opportunities.

Sir Hugh Casson: *Conducting the Auction*. Pen and black ink and watercolour, 29·2 × 22·9 cm.

(*Opposite*)
One of the Porters at Christie's Auction Room. A caricature watercolour by the amateur John Nixon (c.1750–1818).

one of the Porters. at Christie's Auction Room

Perhaps the strongest draw of the auction is that with judgement, hard work and luck anyone may be able to snatch something glorious from under the noses of the enemy: and while we are actually bidding everybody else is the enemy – dealers, fellow collectors, ignorant and innocent-seeming passers-by, and above all that charming and so helpful wielder of the hammer on the rostrum, whose job it is to make us pay the highest possible price. Probably the nearest equivalent to a good buy at auction in terms of thrill and satisfaction is to have pulled off a superb coup on the racecourse by a mixture of inside knowledge, close observation in the paddock, timing, and once again great good luck. This sort of thrill, the sheer euphoria of collecting, is generally less powerful in the calm of a gallery than in the heat of the sale room. However, there is considerable satisfaction to be had in the prising of a bargain from a professional who ought to have had a better idea of its true value.

The foregoing has undoubtedly placed too great an emphasis on the adversarial element in picture-buying. It is most important to remember that until the moment comes to make a bid or strike a bargain, everyone should be treated as a source of information and an ally, if not as a bosom friend. A good dealer or a good auctioneer, like any other salesman, wishes to do the best by his stock or the property of his client. At the same time he hopes to encourage you to return for more. It is not in his long-term interest to palm you off with something dubious merely to get it off his hands.

So at a gallery if you want to know more, ask the owner or assistant; if you are puzzled or dubious at an auction view, summon the expert, who is often the cataloguer. Provided that you do not give away too many of your own secret interests and theories, anything that they can tell you can only be of benefit – and it could well save you from the consequences of following a disastrous hunch. In these circumstances certainly be cautious, but do not be shy: it is their job to give you the information you need.

A good picture can be found anywhere and at any time, and the eyes and ears of the dedicated collector must always be open. On a bus or in a pub or bar an informative conversation may be overheard. In the house of an acquaintance or friend you may find just what you have been looking for – but be careful that a tactless approach does not just lose you a friend but make an enemy for life: passions can be strong in this game. Never assume that a quest or a source is hopeless. I have been dragged all protesting into a country antiques fair that I just knew, from previous experience, would be full of over-priced rubbish, and have come away chastened but triumphant with some of the best buys of my life.

In March 1965 Rembrandt's *Portrait of his Son Titus* made what was then the highest price ever paid for a work of art, 760,000 guineas. What was overlooked in the newspaper headlines was how the painting first came to England. In the early nineteenth century the London dealer George Barker was benighted in a tumbledown farmhouse near the Hague having missed the boat to England. He was shown to a dark bedroom, and the next morning he woke up to find the portrait hanging at the end of his bed. Apparently the farmer was only too glad to have it taken away for

Portobello Road in London is renowned for its antique and 'junk' market.

him, and merely charged what must then have been a rather expensive one shilling for bed and breakfast. If you or I woke up to find such a thing staring at us, would we not probably dismiss it as a copy or reproduction? But who knows . . .

The point, then, is that however often we are disappointed, we must never overlook either the most obvious or the least likely sources of supply.

Having said this, and once again given the physical scope of this book, I can only discuss in detail the ways in which one can get the best service out of a few of the more obvious sources.

Every trade has its jargon, and the art business is no exception, so before going on a buying spree, and especially before going to an auction as an active participant, it is as well to get some of the terms and phrases clear in the mind. Even in such a small language as this there are sub-dialects and local usages, and in the following list I have tried to indicate the words which mean different things when used by a dealer or by an auctioneer. Like other languages and dialects this one is constantly changing and developing, and usages can quickly become out of date: the phrase 'dealers' ring', for example, has now entered standard English, but is distinctly *passé* among 'the Boys' themselves.

Against you all: a phrase used by an auctioneer to indicate that he has a commission bid which outdoes anything that he has been able to elicit from those actually present in a sale room.

Appraise: the American equivalent of the British 'value'. Appraisals are generally made for one of three purposes: insurance, generally highest because it is the figure for replacement; sale, which is the current market value and is likely to be the most realistic; and probate, which tends to be on the low side because taxes will generally be due on the figure.

A/F: 'as found' (i.e. *caveat emptor*, let the buyer beware). This is rarely applied to pictures, being more generally used of furniture and miscellaneous goods. In the U.S. the equivalent is 'as is'.

Barker: the British term for someone who sniffs out goods for a dealer.

Bid: as in 'I am bid' from the auctioneer on announcing a lot. This does not mean that someone extravagant in the room has plunged in at a high level to start the bidding, but that the auctioneer has at least two commission bids on the book, and probably a reserve, and wishes to shorten the proceedings.

Bought in: the auctioneer and his client will usually set a reserve price beneath which a lot may not be sold. The auctioneer will bid as if he was the owner until that figure is reached, as long as there is any competition. If that figure is not reached, the lot is 'bought in' by the auction house on behalf of the owner, to whom it is then returned.

Boys: the British cant phrase for the dealers who form the regular ring in a sale room.

Buyers' Premium: a surcharge levied on the buyers at an auction in many parts of Britain, Europe and America. It may well be 10 per cent of the successful bid, so for heaven's sake take it into account. Any good auctioneer will have a notice in the room or a statement in the catalogue specifying his rate of premium or the lack of it. In the U.S., law requires that notice of a premium be given in advance both as a written notice and verbally by the auctioneer.

Clerk: the bumptious, grumpy, or merely confident-looking chap sitting next to an auctioneer at a slightly lower level. Do not be put off or intimidated by him, since he is actually one of the most important people in the room. Like the auctioneer he will know all the regular attenders, and he may execute bids for leading dealers and collectors who cannot be present. He may also act for you, if you make a friend of him. Since he is very experienced this can be sensible, but not all auctioneers allow their staff to bid.

The term is not used in the U.S. There, members of the staff, sometimes called 'order bid representatives', are seated at a desk or stand near the auctioneer. They execute left bids and, often, reserves, and handle telephone bids during the sale. There is never a charge to the bidder for this service. Bids coming from these representatives, generally younger members of the staff, are often called by the auctioneer as 'at the desk'.

Closed Sale: this really only applies to the traditional sales in Japan at which only registered dealers are allowed to take part.

Commissaire-Priseur: a French auctioneer. He is basically both a legal functionary of the state and a member of a closed medieval guild. His functions are to gather the properties which are to be sold and to wield the hammer, but he does not catalogue or value them. This is the job of the 'expert', who is generally a dealer working in harness with the Commissaire. In general the inexperienced, whether expert or no, should not participate personally in French auctions.

Commission Bid: in America this is known as the 'order bid', and in Britain it is also referred to as 'a bid on the book'. It means that someone who cannot attend a sale has left a bid with the auctioneer, and it often explains the auctioneer's practice of bidding 'off the wall'. It may also be executed by the clerk.

Contents: a contents sale is one held on the vendor's premises, at which everything on offer should come from the same source. It is otherwise known as a 'house sale', and basically everything must go. It is worth looking out for bought in lots on these occasions, since anything that is left over may well be an embarrassment to the auctioneers and to the vendors or their executors. However, as a general rule, and despite the Mentmore example given earlier, prices tend to be higher than they should be at contents and house sales, purely because everyone thinks that their day out must be crowned with a bargain.

Estimate: the pre-sale estimate is the informed guess of the cataloguer as to the likely price that a lot will fetch at auction. Until you know your cataloguers, be wary of taking estimates as more than a guide-line. Be particularly wary of anything too wide, such as 'from £50 to £200' or '£5,000 to £10,000', which can easily be explained away afterwards if the lot has made much more or much less.

Étude: a partnership of Commissaires-Priseurs, which is the nearest French equivalent to an auction house, although a closer parallel in business terms would be a practice of doctors.

Expert: in French this means the cataloguer and valuer of a sale. In English it merely means someone whose job it is to know, but who should often know better. In the U.S. the British auction houses have introduced the term but it has met with only limited success. The usual American term is 'specialist', and at Christie's South Kensington 'technician'.

Fine: in terms of an auction catalogue this means a little better than average. It is a category that is well worth watching since there may be unrecognized bargains in it. On this scale *'important'* tends to mean expensive, and *'highly important'* very expensive, although these labels are being used less and less.

Every painting that passes through the sale rooms should be carefully examined before the catalogue entry is drawn up.

Folio: 'in the folio' refers in British auctions to unframed watercolours and drawings that are displayed for viewing in paper folders or solander boxes.

Household Effects: the junk end of a contents or house sale. Always check, since this dismissive category may include prints and pictures from spare or servants' bedrooms. Two of the rarest Goya prints to come on the market in recent decades were found just before such a sale being used as lining-paper in a chest of drawers from the staff quarters.

Knockout: See *ring.*

Knocker: a low species of dealer in Britain who calls on the unwary and usually elderly and removes their possessions for a fraction of the true value by a mixture of charm and veiled threat. Traditionally in England the practice has been held to centre on such sea-side resorts as Brighton and Torquay, where there are many elderly and decreasingly wealthy inhabitants. The knocker may offer over the odds for a piece of real rubbish, and then smoothly offer to take away something really good to get it out of your way. If such a plague should visit you, do not let it get beyond the front door, especially if it comes in a pair. Stand up to it, and more often than not it will slink away. It is essential to be firm since once you have agreed to part with something there is no sure legal remedy.

Market Overt: It is unlikely that you will need to know this, but it could save you much grief to be aware of it. Under the property laws of England anything that is sold by market overt, that is to say publicly and between the hours of sunrise and sunset, as in a street market or at a public auction, cannot be recovered, even if it is subsequently proved to have been stolen, provided that the immediate vendor was acting in ignorance. A shop does not count as market overt unless open to the street, so a dealer will have to refund your money and stand the loss if he has unwittingly sold you stolen goods, but not so an auctioneer or a market trader. A few years ago a case hinged on whether a market sale had taken place before sunrise, and since it had, the original owner recovered his stolen candelabrum.

Order Bid: see *commission bid.*

Off the Wall: in British usage an auctioneer takes bids 'off the wall' when he is bidding on behalf of the vendor – that is to say below the reserve price or executing a commission bid, and when there is only one bidder in the room. With movements of the head he will pretend that there is actually a second bidder present. The phrase has a pejorative ring to it, but the practice is justified in these circumstances. However, an auctioneer would be guilty of grave misconduct if he were to manufacture bids off the wall when there was no reserve or commission, merely to extort more from an inattentive genuine bidder.

Francisco de Goya y Lucientes: *A Young Woman in a Trance*. *c*.1780(?). Crayon lithograph, L. 14·4 × 16·1 cm., S. 26·8 × 22·1 cm.

A particularly rare lithograph of the type found lining a chest of drawers.

On the Hammer: this phrase means that the auctioneer has noticed a late bid just as he was bringing down the hammer. He is quite at liberty to re-open the bidding from that point – although there may well be objections from the person who thought that he had secured the object.

Paddle: in many American sales, and at some of the grander country-house sales in Britain and Ireland, you may be issued on arrival with a paddle, which is like a pingpong bat with a number on it, and made to register, giving your name and establishing credit. This shortens the proceedings, since when you make a successful bid you have only to display the number, rather than wait for a runner to take your name and address.

Parcel: in British sales of drawings, watercolours and prints, unframed items which are not valuable enough to be offered on their own and which come from the same vendor, may be lumped together in a 'parcel' to form a viable lot. They tend to be catalogued with the minimum of detail, and unconsidered treasures can sometimes be discovered among them.

Plus one: a most important concept for anyone using an agent at an auction, or leaving a commission bid. Most people tend to think in terms of round figures, so, if you can afford it, you should try to make your upper limit an odd one: £110 rather than £100, and so on. You would be very cross with yourself if someone else secured your heart's lust at £110.

Private Treaty: a sale negotiated between a willing buyer and a willing seller, such as a deal with the government to avoid death duties, or one between relatives dividing an estate.

Private View: as it affects commercial exhibitions this will be discussed in the following section on dealers. It is also used at both commercial galleries and institutions for evening views which are open only to members of an interested group or society, and at which the catalogues may be sold on behalf of a charity. The equivalent U.S. term is 'preview'.

Ring: the commonly accepted term for a group of dealers or other interested parties who attend an auction having agreed that only one of them shall bid for any one lot, so that the competition is lessened; they then hold a private sale of their own at which the goods are re-distributed and the difference between the first sale price and the second is ultimately shared out between the participants (the 'settle-ment'). In English law this is an offence, but it is a difficult one to prove, since 'the Boys' must be caught red-handed during the secondary 'knockout'.

In the sub-dialect used by the staff at Sotheby's, 'ring' can be ambiguous, since there it also refers to the horseshoe of green baize-covered tables at the centre of the sale room at which the top dealers and collectors usually sit so as to get a good last-minute look at the lots as they come up.

Runner: another word with two meanings. As used by a dealer it refers to someone who is in the trade but has no premises of his own, and who 'runs' goods from one dealer or shop to another. Many respected names in the business started in this way. Some of these runners are really barkers, since they supply only one established trader; others will hurry about trying to make a percentage wherever it is to be found. Do not despise them. A good collector should ensure that reliable runners ring him up first. In the U.S. they are often known as 'scouts'.

In the dialect of some London auction houses the word means someone entirely different; the trainee who is deputed to collect names and addresses, and to watch out for overly cautious bidders at a sale. He, too, is worth befriending, since he may be the cataloguer of tomorrow. In some auction houses this junior is referred to as a 'spotter'.

Season: traditionally the British auction season runs from late September until the beginning of July, with a brief Christmas break, but more and more houses sell throughout the year.

Settlement: see *ring.*

Trade Discount: unless you have established your credentials by buying a considerable amount from a dealer, do not try to claim a trade discount. You are a collector not a dealer. If you are offered one by someone who knows you and your form well, take it as a compliment.

Underbidder: when you are studying the prices, it is almost as important to know who just failed to buy something as who actually bought it. If something has gone for a huge price to a supposed expert, was the underbidder equally knowledgeable?

View: as I hope this book will show, this is the most important part of an auction. Viewing days will usually be on two or three working days before the actual sale. Get there as early as possible, because this will give you a chance to check out the claims made in the catalogue and your own hunches.

In the U.S. 'the view' is 'the exhibition'. The time assigned to it can be from a week or more to one day, so it is important to find out from the printed catalogue or by telephoning the auction house when the sale will be on exhibition.

Withdrawn: occasionally journalists assume that 'withdrawn' is synonymous with 'bought in'. It is not. A withdrawn lot has been removed from the sale before it begins either by a vendor who has had second thoughts or by the auction house because of doubts as to its ownership or attribution. A bought in lot has failed to reach its reserve. It can be worth enquiring about both after the sale.

Wrong-footed: you are 'wrong-footed' if you have entered the bidding at a sale at a point which makes it impossible for you to buy your lot exactly on your upper limit. If, for instance, you have a limit of £100 and the bidding is increasing by £10 a time, you must obviously be sure that you start at £60 rather than £70. An inexperienced auctioneer may also be 'wrong-footed' when bidding up to a reserve or on behalf of a commission, and he will usually try to rectify the situation by making a half-bid, that is to say £95 rather than the expected £100, before it is too late. If you are sure that this is what is happening, make one more bid, even if it is over your original limit, since this could mean that you have beaten the reserve and that there is no other competition. If you suspect that your lot has actually been bought in at the sale, by all means check up with the auctioneers afterwards. It is possible that the owner will now be willing to accept an offer – perhaps even less than the original reserve.

The Dealers

Having familiarized ourselves with some of the terms let us now take a stroll around a few galleries and study the inhabitants. Picture dealers come in all shapes from the drunk and jovial to the ascetic and aesthetic by way of both the suave and the shambolic. Some are formidably erudite and others crassly ignorant. There are bores and splendid eccentrics. The only common thread is a strong individualism.

Perhaps the most serious mistake that the beginner can make is to assume that all dealers are automatically crooks out to chisel him at every opportunity. Any dealer who does have this attitude to his public is unlikely to stay in business for very long. An actual client must be encouraged to return whenever the fit is on him and his purse permits; a potential client must not be repelled at the first attempt to clamber on board. You must not be put off by the size of a dealer's mark up if it is justified by the quality of the object. If, for instance, you knew that he had paid a mere £5 for an unrecognized Turner watercolour, and then sold it for £10,000, you should not condemn him for profiteering, but rather cultivate him as a man of proven professional skill. A picture dealer is, or should be, a professional in the same way as a surgeon, a lawyer, a hat-maker or a garage mechanic is, and he must be expected to profit by his specialist knowledge. It is up to you to know that he is not making an unjustifiable profit by being constantly aware of current prices in your field. At this stage in your collecting career any good dealer is likely to know a great deal more than you do. He will often also know more than the seemingly grander and more confident experts at museums and auction houses. The reason for this is obvious: he has to back his eye with his own money. The others may lay their reputations on the line, but not, in the short term, their livelihoods.

Thus one of the first things that a tyro collector should try to do, having decided on his field, is to establish good relations with a reputable dealer. Not everyone can spare the time to attend all views and sales, and not everyone cares to rely on their own unsupported judgement in the early stages. Ask around, as you would if you were looking for an accountant; visit all the galleries that you can; find out whose taste, personality and usual stock best accord with you and your needs.

A good dealer as your agent can be your ears as well as an invaluable lens for your eye. His information-gathering network is likely to be much wider and more efficient than your own. You may hear of a potential bargain in an obscure sale: he is likely to be aware of it already and can tell you something of its history and quality, and whether it really is worth chasing. He should know whether something that seems fresh to you has already been offered around the trade, or whether the relevant experts have expressed doubts or approval. He is in a position to assess the likely strength of any potential opposition. Above all, he can help to develop – but must never be allowed to form – your taste.

Through negotiating skill, experience and trade discounts an agent may be able to secure something for you more cheaply than you could get it for yourself, even allowing for his commission. This naturally varies. In London it is generally between 5 and 8 per cent, and in America it may be 10 per cent. Having bought the object he can also deal with subsequent irritations such as restoration, re-framing, insurance, export licences and shipping. In some countries, notably France, Italy and Japan, the complexities of the system are such that it is most unwise to attempt to buy at auction except through an experienced agent.

Charles Turner: *Paul Colnaghi* (1751–1833). Drawing in brush and sepia, 30·5 × 38 cm. London, P. & D. Colnaghi & Co. Ltd.

Paul Colnaghi was probably the first of the modern style of art dealer, and his business still survives in Bond Street, London.

Dealers, like other tradesmen, tend to flock together, whether in St. James's (left) or Portobello (below).

As we shall see shortly, such an agent need not be a dealer, but as often as not a dealer is the best person to advise you and act for you in the early days of your career.

In fact many dealers do not make it easy for a stranger to approach them. A good number, whether in London's art dealing square mile between Oxford Street and Pall Mall, or in Paris, live in apparently forbidding seclusion on the first floor. There you will find them, or rather their well-bred receptionists, sitting behind imposing, if often reproduction, knee-hole desks, in semi-darkness and a heavy silence broken only by telephone calls of a dauntingly esoteric nature. Dealers and receptionists who live in basements behave in exactly the same manner. The grander folk at ground level can naturally be the most daunting of all.

Do not be put off. There is a beneficial aspect to such seeming haughtiness. More often than not you will be left alone to enjoy or surreptitiously sneer at your own pace without the intrusions of salesmanship. This last is a point which should always be borne in mind by Americans buying in Britain. In a New York gallery the dealer and his staff may give the same initial impression, but they will be at your elbow immediately with offers of help or information. The British buyer can be, but must not be, just as put off by this as the American in London who feels that he is being ignored. In either case, ask for information when you are ready.

Haggling, except between dealers, is not very much in the western tradition. While one may gently enquire whether this is the best price that the dealer can do, one should be prepared to accept the answer as final. If there is nothing for you on your first visit to a gallery, but you feel that there might be in the future, do not leave without making yourself known. Stop for a chat about your interests and the state of the market, and leave your name and address. This should mean that you will be contacted if anything in your line turns up, and that you will receive advance notice of exhibitions and cards for private views. One of the most valuable tools of any trader is his contact list, so you should make sure that you are on it.

Sadly, private views have lost some of their point in recent years. All too often they take place on the evening of the first day of an exhibition, rather than on the night before the official opening. It has become common practice, too, for a dealer to sell a certain percentage before the show goes up at all, so as to cover himself. It can be very irritating to think yourself among the privileged few and then find that the best things have gone already. If you find that your man acts in this way, all you can do is ring him up and express interest as soon as you receive the catalogue or card through the post. A dealer who is showing in his own shop has less excuse for this, but one who has rented the space has his hire charges to consider.

On the morning of the opening of a major show there will often be a queue of dealers or their runners waiting outside from a dauntingly early hour. They usually know exactly what they want, and rush in to secure it as soon as the doors open. If you can face a long and perhaps cold wait in what may feel like the middle of the night, you should make the effort and join them. It is all very friendly, with thermos flasks and gossip on the go — but do not be caught off guard when the charge is sounded.

The private view is still worth going to, even if you no longer automatically get first pick of what is on offer. Often all present (except of course the owner) appear to be totally uninterested in whatever is on the walls. On the other hand even if you share this view of the pictures, you might get decent champagne and smoked salmon, and you may find that an awful lot of the gossip has a bearing on your concerns. The art world is tight-knit and inward-looking, and it dearly loves to talk about itself. There should certainly be people present from whom you can learn much, even if only what to avoid. On the whole, picture buyers and dealers are friendly people and very willing to share their knowledge with an enthusiastic beginner. (This is particularly true of my own preferred field of English watercolours.) The golden rule of the collector is to remain friends with everybody. Anyone may happen on something good, and it is essential that they give you first refusal.

A good early relationship with a dealer can also pay dividends at a later stage. If you find that you are dissatisfied with what you bought, or if it is not what it was claimed to be, a dealer is much more likely to take it back than would be an auctioneer, who is after all only an agent. When you need a valuation for insurance or other purposes he will provide it with the minimum of fuss. Also, should you wish to sell quickly, a serious dealer is always more than happy to buy back his old stock. After all, if it was good when he sold it to you, it should still be good, and time will have made it more valuable. If a dealer seems unwelcoming when you wish to sell back your purchases, be very wary of him in the future.

So the basic rules are, be cautious and well-mannered; only be secretive when it is absolutely necessary; and always remember that *caveat emptor* means you.

Auctions and Auctioneers

Caveat emptor is a principle which must be applied even more strongly when buying at auction. Most good auction houses offer some sort of a guarantee, but these are very carefully worded and should be studied with the strictest attention before a purchase is made. Even in the case of a deliberate forgery, the onus of proof is on the buyer. I will quote the relevant conditions of sale from the London catalogues of Christie's and Sotheby's, and you will see for yourself why they should be studied before, rather than after, the sale.

Christie's

6

a. All statements in the Catalogues, advertisements or brochures of forthcoming sales as to any of the matters specified in (b) and (c) below are statements of opinion and are not, nor are they to be relied upon as statements or representations of fact. Illustrations in the Catalogues, advertisements or brochures of forthcoming sales are solely for the guidance of intending purchasers and are not to be relied upon in terms of tone or colour or necessarily to reveal imperfections in any lot. Intending buyers must satisfy themselves by inspection or otherwise as to all such matters, as to the physical description of any lot and as to whether or not any lot has been repaired.

b. Neither the Seller nor Christie's are responsible for the correctness of any statement as to the authorship, origin, date, age, attribution, genuineness or provenance of any lot, or any other errors of description.

c. Neither the Seller nor Christie's are responsible for any faults or defects in any lot.

d. Neither the Seller nor Christie's nor any person in their employ, make or have any authority to make any representation or warranty nor are they responsible for any representation or warranty, or for any statement in the Catalogues, advertisements or brochures of forthcoming sales or photographs therein.

7

a. Notwithstanding any other terms of these Conditions, if within 21 days after the sale Christie's have received from the Buyer of any lot notice in writing that in his view the lot is a deliberate forgery and within 14 days after such notification the Buyer, where the lot has been taken away, returns it to Christie's in the same condition as at the time of sale and within a reasonable period thereafter by producing evidence, the burden of proof to be upon the Buyer, satisfies Christie's that considered in the light of the entry in the Catalogue the lot is a deliberate forgery then the sale of the lot will be rescinded and any purchase price paid refunded.

(*Above, left*) A watercolour painted *c*.1877 of the interior of the London picture dealers Thomas Agnew and Son (William Agnew seated).

Comparatively little has changed in the downstairs gallery at Agnew's. The contemporary photograph (below) is taken from the side by the windows in the watercolour.

b. 'A deliberate forgery' means a lot made or substantially made with an intention to deceive, when considered in the light of the entry in the Catalogue, and which at the date of the sale had a value materially less than it would have had if it had been in accordance with that description.

Sotheby's
16 Liability of Sotheby's and Sellers.

(a) Goods auctioned are usually of some age. All goods are sold with all faults and imperfections and errors of description. Illustrations in catalogues are for identification only. Buyers should satisfy themselves prior to sale as to the condition of each lot and should exercise and rely on their own judgement as to whether the lot accords with its description. Subject to the obligations accepted by Sotheby's under this Condition, none of the seller, Sotheby's, its servants or agents is responsible for errors of description or for the genuineness or authenticity of any lot, no warranty whatever is given by Sotheby's, its servants or agents, or any seller to any buyer in respect of any lot and any express or implied conditions or warranties are hereby excluded.

(b) Any lot which proves to be a "deliberate forgery" may be returned by the buyer to Sotheby's within 5 years of the date of the auction in the same condition in which it was at the time of the auction, accompanied by a statement of defects, the number of the lot, and the date of the auction at which it was purchased. If Sotheby's is satisfied that the item is a "deliberate forgery" and that the buyer has and is able to transfer a good and marketable title to the lot free from any third party claims, then sale will be set aside and any amount paid in respect of the lot will be refunded, provided that the buyer shall have no rights under this Condition if:

(i) the description in the catalogue at the date of the sale was in accordance with the then generally accepted opinion of scholars and experts or fairly indicated that there was a conflict of such opinion; or

(ii) the only method of establishing at the date of publication of the catalogue that the lot was a "deliberate forgery" was by means of scientific processes not generally accepted for use until after publication of the catalogue or a process which was unreasonably expensive or impractical; or

(c) A buyer's claim under this Condition shall be limited to any amount paid in respect of the lot and shall not extend to any loss or damage suffered or expense incurred by him.

(d) The benefit of this Condition shall not be assignable and shall rest solely and exclusively in the buyer who, for the purpose of this Condition, shall be and only be the person to whom the original invoice is made out by Sotheby's in respect of the lot sold.

The terms of warranty are different for both Sotheby's and Christie's in their American operations because they are governed by municipal and state law, and in New York City also fall under the jurisdiction of the Department of Consumer Affairs. When the houses hold sales out of New York State, as they occasionally do, the Conditions of Sale have to be changed to reflect state and local laws although there is rarely a change in the sections concerning guarantee of authenticity.

Christie's New York warrants

For a period of six years from the date of sale that any article in this catalogue unqualifiedly stated to be the work of a named author or authorship is authentic and not counterfeit. The term 'author' or 'authorship' refers to the creator of the article or to the period, culture, source, or origin, as the case may be, with which the creation of such article is identified in the description of the article in this catalogue.

Except as specifically provided in Christie's 'Limited Warranty', all property is sold 'as is' and neither the seller not Christie's makes any express or implied warranty or representation of any kind or nature with respect to the property, and in no event shall they be responsible for the correctness of or be deemed to have made any representation or warranty of merchantibility, description, genuineness, attribution, provenance, or condition concerning the property . . .

Specifically excluded from Christie's Limited Warranty is the following category:

Christie's Limited Warranty does not apply to the identity of the creator of paintings, drawings, graphic art or sculpture before 1870, as the attributions of such identity is based on current scholarly opinion, which may change.

Sotheby's New York conditions of sale relating to warranty are generally the same as Christie's New York, although the wording is different. Works executed before 1870 are excluded from the guarantee, but so also are other objects covered by these headings:

The identification of the periods or dates of execution of the property which may be proven inaccurate by means of scientific processes not generally accepted for use until after publication of the catalogue . . .

Titles or other identification of offered lots or descriptions of physical condition and size, quality, rarity, importance, provenance, exhibitions and literature of historical relevance which information normally appears in lower case type below the bold face heading identifying the authorship.

Conditions of sale should also be read to see what, if any, extras may accompany a successful bid, such as buyers' premium, VAT, or a state or local sales tax. In common with so much else in life, auctions, which used to be simple – you paid what you had bid – have become entangled with governmental bureaucracy, and the small print must always be studied and learned by rote.

By this point, and having read this book from cover to cover, you will of course be fully conversant with the conventional terms in which a picture is catalogued, and you will not have the innocence to complain when what you bought under the heading of 'Rubens' proves to have been painted in 1920. Here, just to remind you, is a list of the various gradations of attribution. It is the one devised by Sotheby's in 1983 and is currently the most elaborate and specific.

Explanation of Cataloguing Terms

Any statement as to authorship, attribution, origin, date, age, provenance and condition is a statement of opinion and is not to be taken as a statement or represenation of fact. Sotheby's reserve the right, in forming their opinion, to consult and rely upon any expert or authority considered by them to be reliable.

1 A picture catalogued with the forename(s) and surname of the painter is in our opinion a work by that artist; e.g. Sir Peter Paul Rubens. When an artist's forename(s) is not known, a series of asterisks, followed by the surname of the artist, whether preceded by an initial or not, indicates that in our opinion the work is by the artist named.

2 A picture catalogued as "Attributed to . . ." is in our opinion *probably* a work by the artist; e.g. Attributed to Sir Peter Paul Rubens.

3 A picture catalogued as "Studio of . . ." is in our opinion a work from the studio of the artist which *may or may not have been executed* under his direction; e.g. Studio of Sir Peter Paul Rubens.

4 A picture catalogued as "Circle of . . ." is in our opinion *a work of the period* of the artist executed under his immediate influence; e.g. Circle of Sir Peter Paul Rubens.

5 A picture catalogued as "Follower of . . ." is in our opinion a work by a painter working *in the artist's style*, contemporary or nearly contemporary, but not necessarily his pupil; e.g. Follower of Sir Peter Paul Rubens.

6 A picture catalogued as "Manner of . . ." is in our opinion a work in a style related to that of the artist, *but of a later date*; e.g. Manner of Sir Peter Paul Rubens.

7 A picture catalogued as "School" accompanied by the name of a place or country and a date means that in our opinion the picture was executed at that time and in that location; e.g. Flemish School, 17th century.

8 A painting catalogued as "After" an artist is in our opinion a copy of any date after a work by that artist; e.g. After Sir Peter Paul Rubens.

9 The term "signed" and/or "dated" and/or "inscribed" means that in our opinion the signature and/or date and/or inscription are from the hand of the artist.

10 The terms ''Bears'' a signature and/or date and/or an inscription means that in our opinion the artist's name and/or date and/or inscription have been added by another hand.

11 All references to signature, inscriptions, and dates refer to the present state of the work.

12 Dimensions are given height before width.

In the U.S. Sotheby's uses an asterisk by the artist's name in catalogue description followed by the statement: 'Authorship: Ascribed to the named artist – subject to the qualifications set forth in the Glossary and Conditions of Sale, front of this catalogue.' The asterisk and statement appear beside most lots.

The glossary printed in the front of the catalogue states as examples of terminology:

a. ''Giovanni Bellini'' – Followed, under the heading ''Authorship'' by the words ''ascribed to the named artist.'' The work is ascribed to the named artist either by an outside expert or by our own staff and such ascription is accepted as reliable by the Galleries. While this is our highest category of authenticity in the present catalogue, and is assigned only upon exercise of our best judgement, no unqualified statement as to authorship is made or intended.

b. Attributed to Giovanni Bellini – In our best judgement, the work can be ascribed to the artist on the basis of style, but less certainty as to authorship is expressed than in the preceding category.

c. Circle of Giovanni Bellini – In our best judgement, a work by an unknown hand closely associated with the named artist.

d. Studio of Giovanni Bellini – In our best judgement, a work by an unknown hand executed in the style of the artist under his direct supervision.

e. School of . . . Follower of Giovanni Bellini – In our best judgement, a work by a pupil or follower of the artist.

f. Manner of Giovanni Bellini – In our best judgement, a work in the style of the artist, but not by him and probably of a later period.

g. After Giovanni Bellini – In our best judgement, a copy of a known work of the artist.

h. Signed – A work which has a signature which in our best judgement is a recognized signature of the artist.

i. Dated – A work which is so dated and in our best judgement was executed at that date.

Let us suppose that you have now spent as much time as possible in reading, studying your field and getting a sense of the market, and that you feel that you are ready to make your first serious foray into the jousting ground of an auction. You have subscribed for the relevant catalogues and a likely one arrives with the breakfast. Run through it rapidly marking lots of potential interest. Check these against the pre-sale estimates, remember that estimates are a better guide to the probable reserve figures than to actual sale price, and note any of these that your experience of previous results and prices tells you is anomalous. A low estimate may indicate that the cataloguer is unaware of recent developments in other sales or dealers' exhibitions, but, on the other hand, a low estimate on something which is fully catalogued as being by a well-known artist may indicate that the lot is in poor condition or has some other drawback. It may be prudence rather than ignorance. Again, you may notice something that the cataloguer seems to have missed, such as the full names behind a series of asterisked initials.

Next you will note the view days, or exhibition days as they are known in the U.S. It has already been implied and must now be emphasized that the view days are the most important part of a sale for the potential buyer. Unless you really know what you are about, you should never bid blind on the strength of a catalogue description. At many sale rooms it is not possible to examine the lots on the day of sale itself, so if you cannot attend the view in person, commission someone whose judgement you trust to go and have a proper look for you.

In any case the view is an education in itself. On the way to it you will probably pass other auctions in progress, if you are at a major house, and you will learn something from even a few moments lounging at these. At a humbler country sale you can find out who else has got wind of anything good. Watch how the dealers handle the objects. They are accustomed to handling expensive objects and are not frightened of them. Where you might be intimidated by a painting worth several thousand pounds and be chary of so much as touching it, they will heave it off the wall and look at the back. They will demand that the porter in attendance takes it out of the frame if necessary, and they will riffle through the portfolios of drawings or prints as if they were daily newspapers. Also, you will notice that unless they are specialists and after only one thing, they will study everything, however trivial the catalogue description may have made it appear. On these occasions you will understand that the good dealer does really earn his money. Museum limp is a well-known complaint, except to medical science; viewing blindness is a similar condition. It is all too easy to pass over a treasure when you have been confronted by nothing but dross for the previous half hour or so.

Use every sense that you have developed so far, and call on every scrap of memory. Then go away and check where necessary. You should have a day or two's grace to do this before the actual sale, and in this you have the advantage over the cataloguer, except where major paintings are concerned. The items which interest you may have been in the sale room warehouse for weeks or months, but the time which the staff can spend in studying any one of them is strictly limited by practical and financial considerations. A cataloguer can rarely give a couple of hours to something which may be worth £50 as it stands, or with further research

£100, since his commission will not justify it. He has dozens of things to look at and identify each day; you have two or three days to find out more about just one or two of them.

If after research and cogitation, you decide that you still want to buy, and you wish to bid for yourself, be sure that you are in good time for the sale, at least until you know the particular lot-rate of the particular auctioneer. Nothing is more frustrating than to arrive just after the relevant fall of the hammer. The pace of sales varies enormously, depending on the experience of the auctioneer and the quality of the lots. A hundred lots of important Old Master paintings may take as long as two hundred lots of run-of-the-mill drawings or miscellaneous properties, since the stakes are higher and the game is played with greater finesse. As a rule of thumb, in a routine sale most London auctioneers average somewhere between 60 and 100 lots an hour. However, even if you know the form of your man, and the lot that you want comes late in the sale, it can be worth your while to arrive at the beginning. You can get the most advantageous position – I generally prefer to stand towards the back on the right-hand side, so as to have a clear view of the auctioneer and the whole room, and also to get a last look at the lots as they come up – and you can get the mood of the day and assess the competition. At large country sales most of the serious dealers who have travelled a long way will usually look in at an early stage, even if they do not intend to bid until much later, and it is as well to know who is there.

However, let us return to London and 'Eleven o'clock precisely', as the catalogues put it. Auction sales are many things, and among them theatre. At first the audience will be gently milling about and chatting, and a few porters and runners will be hovering on the fringes of the room like gnomish usherettes. Then the clerk arrives, perhaps with a junior, armed with his book, which records almost all the information that the auctioneer will have in front of him, except the names of the vendors and the reserve prices, together with lists of his commission bids. The crowd begins to sit down, and, star-like, the auctioneer arrives and ascends the rostrum. 'Good morning ladies and gentlemen; lot 1. May I say £20?' The very first lots are likely to be in the nature of a warm-up routine, although in drawings sales, when albums and large parcels may be involved – unframed lots are usually offered before framed – they can cause considerable excitement.

Some people maintain that the etiquette of the sale room decrees that you should not look round at bidders behind you if you are sitting down. However at least one leading London firm of dealers normally flouts this. Its representatives usually work in tandem, and having seated themselves in their regular spot near the front and to the left, one concentrates on the auctioneer, and the other reports on what is happening to the rear of the room.

An experienced auctioneer with a regular clientele will usually know roughly who is likely to be interested in each lot, and will be looking out for bids from them. This means that as a newcomer you must make your bid clearly so as to be sure of attracting his attention. Maître Rheims, one of the most notable French auctioneers, claimed that he would often know

A corner of a picture warehouse at Christie's in London.

when someone was about to make a bid, because they would show slight signs of agitation during the sale of the previous lot. Certainly, it is very difficult to remain completely calm when you are making your first few bids. Indeed, after some twenty years of it I still find myself becoming nervous as the moment approaches. However, the one thing that need not worry you is the old wives' tale that if you so much as sneeze you will find that something expensive has been knocked down to you. It is the job of the auctioneer to distinguish genuine bids from twitches, and if he is in any doubt he will ask you directly.

Out of politeness he will remain with the original contestants until one or both drops out, so you may not be able to get into the bidding when you want, or indeed at all. Once you are in, make you gestures clearly – but not too flamboyantly, which will mark you as a novice – especially when you want to stop. By this time you will have acquainted yourself with the probable sequence of bids – 2 : 5 : 8 : 10 : 12 : 15 : 18 : 20 : 25 : 30 : perhaps in tens from 50, twenties from 100 and so on. Some firms will take larger leaps from the start. In any case you must not be surprised if your increment is taken as 100 rather than 50. When you secure your first lot a

The sale of Velázquez's *Juan de Pareja* in 1970. This was the first painting to break the million pound barrier at auction. Below the auctioneer are two clerks recording the bids, as well as runners, press officers and other auction house staff.

runner will seek you out for your name and address, and on subsequent successes the auctioneer should call out your name with the fall of the hammer.

It is not really possible to generalize as to when it is best to enter the bidding, and how fast or slowly you should make your bids. An instant return of bid may give the impression that you are confident and wish to hurry things along, or it may imply to the competition that you are trying to disguise the fact that you have almost reached your upper limit. If you have gathered that you are bidding against a reserve or commission bid, rather than someone else in the room, and you have decided to drop out, take notice if the auctioneer is at particular pains to wheedle another bid from you: 'Against you, sir. One more? Another one, sir?', which may indicate that a last try will pass the reserve. 'Are you all done, then?' means that there has been lively bidding in the room, and he is probably satisfied with the result.

A final point of etiquette: never try to take a peek at someone else's catalogue – or if you do make sure that your are not noticed. This can cause great offence, since he may have marked the lots that he is interested in and noted the limits of his bids. This is why many professionals use a letter/number code of their own. Even if you do not really need one, it adds to the fun to make one up for yourself.

After the sale, or during it if the firm is efficiently computerized, you will have to queue to pay and then to collect your lots. At this point you have no one to blame but yourself if you are surprised by a buyers' premium, sales tax or VAT. Check the lots before you remove them. Funny things have been known to happen between the fall of the hammer and collection. This is another occasion when the use of a dealer as agent can be an advantage. Most firms like immediate payment, and clearance either immediately or within three days. A dealer who is a regular customer can sometimes win you extra time.

A big firm can arrange for packing and transport or shipping on your behalf, and also obtain any necessary licences for you. A smaller one should be able to recommend reliable specialists. Remember that if you do use these services it will possibly be a long time before you receive your purchase, and it just may get damaged in the interim.

If you have failed to secure the lot that you wanted, you need not always despair. If by chance it was bought in, you may be approached by the sale room afterwards to see if you are still interested. In any event it can be efficacious to leave a post-sale offer on a bought-in lot, and this is particularly true when it comes from a deceased estate. Executors are usually under pressure to wind up an estate quickly, and if they have set too high a reserve, they are in a weak position for haggling if it has not been reached.

Again, if you were the underbidder on a lot which contained two or more items, only one of which you really wanted, check with the purchaser afterwards to see if you can come to an arrangement. If the case is the other way about, see if you can off-load the unwanted items on the underbidder, or if the auction house will take them back for a subsequent sale. Deals such as this can best be struck in the nearest pub, where you will probably find most of the dealers and perhaps the auctioneer himself. If you do go there you may also learn the inside stories on anything that puzzled you during the sale itself.

Outside London and in the secondary rooms things tend to be a little less formal, and the auctioneers still sometimes let themselves go in the old manner, insulting the room when the bidding is sluggish and cracking up the goods for all that they are worth, and a good deal more. This is one reason why country sales often take longer, another of course being that they are often general sales, including almost everything, and there are more lots on offer. Just occasionally you may still come across a small concern that insists on payment in cash, which can be awkward when the sale does not finish until after the banks have closed. Country sales are fun, but can be frustrating. You may visit a dozen on the strength of tip-offs and optimistic catalogues before you find anything worth buying, and all too often the big boys have heard about that too. Even so there is always a moment of thrill as one enters a dingy hall for a view: perhaps this is the day of the Great Discovery.

Since the 1960s, when first Sotheby's and then Christie's and Phillips began to expand their operations across the world, the differences in auctioneering practice from country to country have grown less, but many persist, and wherever you come from, you should not assume that things will be just as they would be at home.

As Daniel and Katharine Leab put it in their book *The Auction Companion* (1981): 'the largest and best-known auction houses in the United States are Sotheby's and Christie's, and they speak to the public with an English accent.' Things are very different in the third capital of the western art world, Paris, where the accent is purely Gallic, and no foreign firms are allowed to trespass. Indeed, the Commissaire-Priseur is not allowed to operate outside his own city, which precludes the development in France of auction houses as they are known elsewhere.

The system is reminiscent of the monopolistic medieval city guilds. In Paris the guild is the *Compagnie des Commissaires-Priseurs*, which is made up of some 80 *études*, or practices. Since auctioneering is a branch of property law, the Commissaires are considered legal functionaries and are styled *Maître*. The Compagnie owns the complex of sale rooms at the Hôtel Drouot, and so although each *étude* has its own office, it must hire a room each time it holds a sale. The cataloguing and valuing is done by government-licensed experts, who are often dealers; they are often more important from the buyer's point of view than the Commissaires, and they may work with several of them.

In general a higher percentage of private buyers attend Paris sales than they do elsewhere, but unless you read and speak French well it might be best to act through an agent. The buyers' premium can be up to 16 per cent, with tax. With works by living artists there is also the *droit de suite* to pay: 3 per cent of the hammer price which goes to the artist himself or his heirs. When a major or even minor work is sold, it may be pre-empted by a French national gallery or institution, which means that the gallery takes it at the hammer price, and the person who thought he had secured it must smile sweetly. Even if you feel daunted by the thought of buying, you

The entrance to the complex of sale rooms operated by the Compagnie des Commissaires-Priseurs in Paris.

should always visit the Drouot when in Paris, since anything may be jumbled up in there, from great Old Masters to bankrupt stock. Paris sales are usually smaller and more general than British or American. If you want modern works, do not overlook Maître Blache at Versailles, just outside the jurisdiction of the Compagnie. Paris sales and results are listed in the weekly *Gazette de l'Hôtel Drouot*.

The French system thus excludes foreign auctioneers and explains why the English houses are so active in Switzerland, and why Sotheby's operate in Monaco. By Monegasque law, foreigners may organize sales in the Principality, and even take the bids, but a Monegasque auctioneer must actually bring down the hammer.

In Switzerland the important sales, whether organized by the multi-nationals or by the locals such as Dobiaschofsky and Kornfeld in Berne, Fischer in Lucerne, and Koller in Zurich, take place in massive binges over several days in the spring and autumn. The best-known of the locals for paintings and prints are Koller and Kornfeld. You should note that in the Swiss tradition many auctioneers are also dealers, so your man may be offering his own stock. This is also often the case in West Germany and sometimes in Ireland.

The Germans, too, go in for massive multi-session affairs in spring and autumn, and among the best for pictures are Dorling and Hauswedell & Nolte in Hamburg, Roland A. Exner in Hannover, Lempertz in Cologne, Karl & Faber and Neumeister in Munich, and Fritz Nagel and Gus Schiele in Stuttgart. In Austria the auction house for pictures is the old-established Dorotheum in Vienna, which has a deservedly high reputation. Italian auctions should not be contemplated except by the most foolhardy foreigner.

In Ireland, both North and South, auctioneering is the natural way to sell things. Most houses and other forms of property are auctioned, with the result that many estate agents hold chattels sales. Many dealers, particularly along the Quays in Dublin, will also hold regular sales of their stock. The most eminent of the conventional auction houses is James Adam & Sons of Dublin, which operates in a gentle and gentlemanly way, much as did the English houses before they added modern marketing methods. Sotheby's and Christie's both handle country house sales, but be warned: these tend to be very expensive, although immensely enjoyable, affairs. The refreshment tents are among the best in the world, and often the only bargains to be had are the lots at the end of a long morning session when most people have retired to the Guinness and salmon.

Belgian sales are often of good quality, but be sure that you do your sums correctly since VAT, the buyers' premium and taxes are all high. If you are exporting your purchases all the taxes may not apply to you, but you may have to pay and then wait for the refund to work its way back through the bureaucracy.

In the Netherlands the scene is now dominated by the multinationals, but Paul Brandt is a force to be reckoned with. Dutch sales tend to concentrate on their own artists, so works by foreign painters can sometimes be had reasonably. The 'Dutch', or descending-bid auction, by the way, seems only ever to have been practised in sales of flowers.

Picture dealers may be found in virtually any locality – city, town or village. This shop and gallery is on the Quays in Dublin.

Another area where it is worth looking out for foreign works is Scandinavia, especially Denmark and Sweden. Many Swedes seem to have collected middle-of-the-road nineteenth-century British paintings, and these are coming back onto the market. The most notable firms are Bukowskis and Stockholms Auktionsverk in Stockholm, and Göteborgs Auktionsverk in Göteborg. In Denmark the leader is Arne Bruun Rasmussen, and others include Kunsthallens Kunstauktioner in Copenhagen, Nellemann & Thomsen in Aarhus and Børge-Nielsen in Vejle.

With regard to the further flung parts of the world it is worth noting that the Japanese system of the closed auction, that is, one restricted to registered dealers only, is gradually giving way before the invasion of the multinationals, also that in Argentina sales are often conducted by banks.

Just as the visitor to Britain must not forget that there are several hundred antiques and fine arts auctioneers, and not just the internationally known firms, so too the traveller in North America must not be blinded by the glamour of the multinationals and overlook the many reputable native firms. A good source book for the beginner is Susan Wasserstein, *Collectors' Guide to U.S. Auctions* (New York: Penguin Books, 1981), which lists and discusses more than 300 firms and gives practical information concerning specialities, credit, hours, the frequency of auctions, etc.

At several points in the foregoing notes I have implied that buyers are most concerned with the artists or paintings of their own countries. This is a good general principle to follow. If you want American works, look for them outside the United States, where they are expensive. In the same way the British know all about their own Victorians, but have little interest in other European nineteenth-century schools. But wherever you buy, be sure that you understand the local regulations about export before you bid.

Earlier I mentioned the advantages of using a professional dealer as a buying agent. Should you feel that this is too limiting and that it ties you too closely to one, possibly biased, source of supply, then you might find that another essential art world figure could prove to be the ideal adviser. This is the picture restorer. He must be sought out in the same way as you would a good dealer or other trustworthy expert, namely by word of mouth and personal recommendation. An experienced restorer should have acquired a particularly intimate knowledge of painting and paintings, since his physical contact with them is closer than that of almost anyone else except the original artist. He is not necessarily creative, but he is an expert craftsman, and he sees and handles a great deal, both good and bad.

Using a restorer as an agent is particularly valuable when you are thinking of buying at auction. For the most part, and for obvious reasons of expense, auctioneers do not have paintings cleaned or restored before they offer them for sale (in contrast to dealers, who will usually have had their stock attended to before it goes on exhibition). Thus if you see something that is damaged, or merely dirty, at an auction view, you need to know how much it will cost to have it put right, and if it is worth undertaking at all, before you decide how much you are going to bid. The experts from the sale room can help and advise you in many ways, but rarely in this, since they have so little personal experience of what can or cannot be done, or of how much it is likely to cost.

Most restorers will be happy to accompany you to a view, or to view for you, and just as a dealer who is acting as your agent will not usually charge you commission unless he has actually succeeded in buying on your behalf, so a restorer will generally charge only for the subsequent work and not for doing your bidding. However, if you have sent either a dealer or a restorer to several abortive sales, where the pictures were either not worth bidding for, or were more expensive than you could afford, you must expect him to charge you for his wasted time and his expenses, if any.

Buying Direct

One rather important person has been largely ignored so far in this book, and indeed often seems to be overlooked by people writing about or discussing the art world. This is the artist. Sometimes one almost gets the impression that a painting only becomes art (or rather Art) after the death of the embarrassing and intrusive fellow who has created it.

Certainly, the relationship between an artist and a gallery owner who is trying to promote his work is by no means always an easy one. Artists, sometimes rightly, often regard the dealers who are their marketing agents as no more than parasites, battening on to pure creative genius. Dealers handling contemporary works can, sometimes rightly, feel that artists are impractical and demanding egotists who have no idea of the amount of expense and skill needed to persuade the hard-headed world to buy their vision of it. Unfortunately, there is often wrong on both sides.

A good commercial dealer in contemporary art needs to be a successful talent spotter, and the relationship between him and his artist can be a very good one. A young painter may have to work at one painting or the makings of an exhibition over many months, during which no funds are coming in to pay the basic bills of living. The dealer, if he is to be of any use, can guarantee the funds which ensure that the work is carried out without worry and interruption, as well as possessing the knowledge to market the results successfully. Although one can discount a good many of the horror stories told by artists about the ways in which their dealers have treated them, one must also understand that very few artists have the time or ability to be their own dealers. It is not surprising that creator and salesman often fail to understand each other.

If such a relationship between a painter and his dealer is bad, neither of them is likely to give much thought to the wants of the ultimate buyer. However, the astute collector can turn the situation to his advantage. If you have a passion for the work of a living painter, and he is not already hugely grand, then try to get to know him. A personal relationship can cut out the middle man – or, increasingly, middle woman. It will also give you the chance to buy sketches and minor works which would not be considered valuable enough to be included in an exhibition, or to commission something that is exactly to your taste. The traditional image of an artist as someone who is not very good at organizing his private and financial life is true more often than not. He is often very willing to take cash from an admirer if the gas bill or the alimony is due, and whatever advance or retainer he may have had from his regular gallery is long spent.

If you are seeking for works of roughly our own time, but not absolutely up to the minute, then study the obituary columns of the newspapers. With the exception of such international giants as Picasso, Braque and Miró, works by painters who have made a good and prosperous living in their day, especially if they were prolific, tend to drop in price immediately after their deaths. The reason for this is that during their lifetime prices have been kept up by their agents and themselves, but within a year or so of their deaths there is often a massive studio sale at which many sketches, unfinished works and discards come onto the market, and the volume is too great for any one market manager to be able to control. Other people think that they may be able to cash in on the publicity, and in general the quality is more variable than before. This means that for several years, in some cases up to about a decade, prices are volatile, but for the most part on the low side. In the field of modern British paintings and drawings good examples in recent years have been the work of Augustus John and Dame Laura Knight. In the international market the same uncertainties and opportunities for the discriminating were noticeable with Picasso prints, although not with his paintings. As always, the essential attribute is discrimination: good works will often be cheap and good artists underpriced, but poor examples and painters may fetch much the same prices, and you must not find that you have chosen the wrong ones when the market sorts itself out again.

Currently sales of an artist's studio are more common in Paris than in London, although Christie's South Kensington and other houses are beginning to adopt the practice. They are still almost unknown in the U.S. Those of less well-known artists are well worth investigating, since the dirty-looking sketches and drawings which come in bundles will often clean and frame amazingly well, as will grubby, unframed canvases. Also, just occasionally, you may come across something by another and altogether better artist jumbled up with the sweepings. Most painters have still more talented friends whose work they admire and acquire and sometimes they never get around to displaying it properly; cataloguers may overlook it too.

The other obvious hope is to acquire the work of a promising artist before he becomes well known. However, it takes a very sure eye to spot the future genius at the beginning of his career, although it is the dream of any collector of contemporary work. Many of us will have been to one of those enviable restaurants where the owner allowed the young and struggling Cubists or whoever to pay for their meals with a canvas or drawing, and whose insurance bill now matches his annual turnover. We tend not to remember those more numerous restaurants where the paintings have been acquired in the same way, but the painters have remained in well-deserved obscurity.

If you do know what you want, however, and it is modern, you might make a point of going to the end of the year shows at the leading art

Augustus John: *Child Study: Pyramus.* c.1908. Pencil, 43 × 20 cm.

The years immediately following the death of a prolific and popular artist are often the best for acquiring his work inexpensively.

Dame Laura Knight: *Clowns and Girl Acrobat on a Horse in a Circus Ring*. Signed and dated 1930. Oil on canvas, 45·7 × 58·4 cm.

Another popular painter whose prices were comparatively low in the years following her death.

(*Below*) David Hockney: *Cleaning Teeth; Early Evening (10 p.m.), W11*. Signed and dated 1962. Oil on canvas, 182 × 122 cm.

Those who spotted the talent of Hockney when he was still at art school and just after are to be congratulated and envied. So many promising students will never be heard of again.

schools. The odds are that your artist, although the undoubted star of his year, will never be heard of again, but it is a comparatively cheap way of buying what you like, and it is just, just, possible that you may hit on the Andy Warhol or David Hockney of the next generation. You will take very much the same gamble if you choose to buy at the Royal Academy, or its equivalents around the world.

The Royal Academy Summer Exhibition

The Royal Academy's section of Burlington House in Piccadilly contains the third most visited art galleries in Britain, as well as the fine Private Rooms, the Academy Schools, the Business Art Galleries and a very useful art reference library which can be consulted without charge. Despite many pleas and promises the Academy has yet to benefit from any regular allocation of public funds, being still essentially a private society run by artists for artists.

While it has a long history of achievement in the field of education and in the mounting of major loan exhibitions, it is perhaps surprising that only about one tenth of the visitors to the Academy each year are drawn in by its own annual Summer Exhibition , which is one of the few occasions when everything is for sale.

The RA was founded in 1768, and a Summer Exhibition has been held every year since, despite wars, rumours of wars, and often impending bankruptcy. In the past, when there was a worthwhile social season in London, the first day of the Summer show was also by tradition its

opening. Everyone from Prime Minister to débutante was seen there, and it was perhaps the one gesture towards culture made by a society usually more concerned with rowing, cricket, racing, balls, routs and, of course, marriages. This alone might well have damned the exhibition in the eyes of the avant-garde, but in this century it has in any case also gained the often justified reputation of being safe, old fashioned and dull, and an irrelevance to anyone really interested in modern painting. The Royal Academicians themselves have all too often been old and backward looking, and the outside exhibitors could seem little better than worthy amateurs.

Any blame for dull worthiness must rest with the Selection Committee of RAs, who by reason of age and eminence may often have been unadventurous in their choice. In recent years, however, notable efforts have been made to enliven the exhibitions and bring them out of the backwaters of British art. One such, which caused a certain amount of healthy internal dissension among the RAs, was the turning over of a complete room to the selection of Peter Blake and the Brotherhood of Ruralists in 1976.

However the avant-garde may view the Summer Exhibition, the number of artists submitting works hung, the number of visitors attending and the number of works sold have continued to rise almost every year. By 1981 the sales totalled £347,268 or 1,510 works, at prices ranging from £12 to £12,000. Usually nearly half the sales are made on one of the two or three private-view days, and the rest over the following three months of the Exhibition's run. Even in 1982, when in common with the trend at other major British museums and galleries, attendance figures dropped noticeably, the number of sales was still increased.

For those who wish to buy contemporary paintings, prints and sculpture of the safer kinds, the Summer show is an unrivalled market place. Buying here should be governed solely by your own taste and pocket. It is unrealistic, as at College Diploma shows, to expect to hit on one of the great artists of the next generation at an embryonic stage: the odds against it are like those against winning a major prize in the football pools. Even the critics are wrong in their predictions more often than not, and it is chastening to re-read the annual reviews predicting glorious careers for those who have never been heard of again. It might, however,

Works being examined at the Royal Academy. Because of the vast numbers of works submitted each year, only a few seconds can be given to each as it passes before the selection committee. Naturally, the process of hanging those selected takes longer.

(*Opposite*)
The interior of Christie's Contemporary Art, London.

if you insist on a cloak of respectability for your purchases, be possible to work out which painters among the outside exhibitors here are likely to win the Academic accolade in the future.

Buying at the show is simple. There are price lists in each room and a central desk for the registration of purchases, and on payment of a deposit representing the Academy's 20 per cent handling commission with VAT, the work is yours, with a red spot to prove it. Thereafter all arrangements are made between the buyer and the artist, which may give you the opportunity to buy further works later. The artists' addresses are given in the catalogue, and if you do not make up your mind before leaving Burlington House, you can contact them or the Secretary later.

Incidentally, do not lose heart if you should see a red spot against a print which interests you, as it may well be one of a limited edition, and other impressions are likely to be available. Prints are also the only works which may have been exhibited elsewhere before appearing here.

The Business Art Galleries

Upstairs from the main galleries is a very different type of selling operation. The Business Art Galleries are a comparatively recent innovation, and the journey to them is worth making for its own sake, since the back staircase is hung with the diploma works of long deceased, and often distinguished RAs.

The Business Galleries deal in original contemporary British work, both paintings and prints. They sell to companies and factories, and the prices are modest. They will also lease paintings and sculpture for limited periods and they will undertake commissions related to a company's special needs – such as portraits of directors or buildings, exclusive editions of prints to mark anniversaries or other special occasions, or even the provision of paintings to fit unusual spaces. Another clever idea is the picture voucher, which can be given as a long-service award or leaving present.

Christie's Contemporary Art

Works by some of the artists represented in the Business Galleries can be seen again at Christie's Contemporary Art at 8 Dover Street, London W1 and at 799 Madison Avenue, New York. This company is a sort of cousin of the auctioneers, since both are subsidiaries of the parent company known as Christie's International. Christie's Contemporary Art deals only with original prints, which, they emphasize, 'are not reproductions of paintings, but original works of art conceived and created by artists who are using their chosen medium to produce effects that could not be achieved in any other way.' As well as comparative unknowns, their stable has included such international giants as Joan Miró and Henry Moore. The firm is different from other dealers in that while recognizing the investment potential of the prints, it deliberately tries to keep their prices low. The plates are destroyed or defaced on the completion of an edition.

4. Prints

The basic commandments for the collector of prints are given in the various introductions to J. H. Slater's *Engravings and their Value*, a classic work which was last re-issued in 1978. Among other wise things Slater and his subsequent editors say:

> Prints have a popular appeal in a way not shared by paintings. This arises firstly from their greater availability, and secondly from their greater range of subject-matter. Collections of prints can be formed on themes and categories in a way quite impossible today with water-colours and oils. [I would contest the inclusion of watercolours, but no matter.]
>
> The practice of buying anything, no matter what, which happens to take the fancy, is not one that can be recommended when the formation of a collection of prints is the primary object in view, though it may, of course, be perfectly legitimate for casual purposes, for instance, as the decoration of the wall of a room . . .
>
> Of course all this activity has given rise to certain commercial practices, such as the deliberate inflation of prices at auction of prints with little or no artistic merit . . . such work is bound to fall in value sooner or later, and the collector who has paid the high price demanded for similar things will be nervous of risking his money again . . .
>
> Go to the best dealers, explain the facts, be guided by their opinion, for no dealer of standing ever yet built up his business by taking advantage of the inexperience of his customers.

Some of the foregoing remarks were written just before the great collapse in the boom market for modern etchings which paralleled the Wall Street Crash and was a direct consequence of it. In the 1920s a number of British artists of great ability, such as Sir David Muirhead Bone (1876–1953) and Sir David Young Cameron (1865–1945), had taken to etching, and their limited editions were taken by investors to be no more nor less than portfolios of stocks and shares. Artistic merit was not a consideration, and when the crash came the good were swept away with the mediocre. It was forty years before the market began to recover.

Perhaps the most misguided publication that I have ever read in this field appeared in 1974. It was called *Pick's World Currency Report*, and it claimed to be a guide to 'alternative investments'. It took a huge subject, such as etchings, and on the strength of the top few auction prices of the current year claimed that the whole market had appreciated by 400 per cent. No attempt was made to compare like with like. It announced that its readership ranged from kings to prostitutes, but in fact the circulation was small, and any such who followed its advice must quickly have become ex-kings and ladies of the night before last. It would not be worth recalling now if other magazines and columns with larger circulations and greater claims to sophistication were not still peddling similar lines. Such things as the alternative investment reports in *The Connoisseur*, the Sotheby Art Index in the U.S. weekly *Barrons*, and the Salomon Brothers report should be read with great caution by anyone who seriously wishes to spend money in the art market.

As a London dealer said of Pick: 'Any attempt to pretend that the art market is merely the stock market by another name will fall down, as Pick's does, because it is impossible to standardize the quality of the items compared.' While the market in prints has a little more in common with stocks and shares than do those in most other forms of original art, it is very foolish to think of prints simply in terms of an investment, as many supposedly intelligent and astute people found in the 1920s and again in the early 1970s.

Original prints are made in many different ways, and since they are usually described very precisely, it is as well to get the terms straight in our minds before we begin to look at them, let alone to buy them.

Aquatint: a method invented in the eighteenth century by the Frenchman Jean Baptiste Le Prince (1733–81). He passed it to the Hon. Charles Greville, who in turn gave it to his friend Paul Sandby in England. To make an aquatint a metal plate is heated and then sprinkled with resin, which will stick to it. It is then bathed in acid, which will bite into any uncovered areas. According to the density of the particles darker or lighter shading is obtained. The effect is much like stipple, and the outlines are then etched or put in with a drypoint. A print is taken and coloured by hand. Aquatint was the ideal method for producing sporting and coaching prints in the nineteenth century.

Artist's Proof: this term should only be used of the one or two examples which are pulled before a limited edition for the benefit of the artist himself. They are usually marked accordingly and signed. It is wrong and misleading to call a mechanical coloured reproduction an artist's proof merely because it is one of a limited and signed edition.

Bite: the action of acid on a plate.

Burr: the rough and raised edges of the furrow made by an incising tool. The burr, as well as the line itself, will hold ink, producing a rich and black impression. It wears away quickly in printing, which is one reason for the desirability of early impressions.

By and After: this indicates that the artist has both made the original design and printed it himself. In the print itself the various degrees of responsibility are often indicated by Latin abbreviations. *Imp*[*ressit*] means that the artist has done his own printing; *pinx*[*it*] or *del*[*ineavit*], that he has only painted or drawn the original, in which case the printer's name will be followed by *f*[*ecit*] or *sculp*[*sit*]. A name followed by *ex*[*udit*] or *exc.* indicates the publisher. *In*[*venit*] means designed by.

Chiaroscuro Woodcut: a technique in which several wood blocks are used to print different colours and give tone. It was particularly popular in sixteenth-century Italy and Germany.

Chromolithography: a method of producing cheap reproductions in large numbers which was popular in the late nineteenth century. Such things do not really count as prints, since the original artist had very little to do with the mechanical process, and it is the watercolour collector rather than the collector of prints who needs to be aware of them as they can occasionally deceive at first glance. The colours and registration are rarely completely true, and the paper has a bobbled appearance like a grainy photograph. Chromolithographs are widely collected in the U.S. for their subjects, which include early city views, Indians and natural history. British subjects are mostly limited to sugary landscapes.

Coloured Reproduction: sometimes misleadingly described as 'artist's proofs' or 'signed proofs', these are really no more and no less valuable than magazine or calendar illustrations which have been signed and numbered by the artist. They are fine for interior decoration, but should not be the concern of the print collector.

Contre-épreuve (counterproof): a reverse impression made by laying a second piece of paper on top of a print when the ink is still wet. Since

William Daniell: *Clovelly on the Coast of North Devon.* Etching and aquatint from *A Voyage Round Great Britain*, 1814–25.

David Hockney: *Pretty Tulips*. 1969.
Lithograph, one of a series of 200, image
and paper sizes, 72·5 × 54·5 cm.

This really is an artist's proof — an
impression pulled for the use of the artist
himself and separate from a numbered
edition. It is not to be confused with the
mechanical coloured reproductions
which are still sometimes sold as 'artists'
proofs'.

the image will be in the same direction as that on the plate, it is a useful
way for an artist to make last-minute corrections. This technique is also
encountered with chalk drawings.

Drypoint: the tool for and technique of drawing directly onto a plate with
a sharp needle. It is often used in conjunction with etching.

Edition: the run of a print published at any one time.

Engraving: the straightforward method of cutting a design into a metal
plate or a wood block so that the lines will retain the ink and the upper
surface remain blank.

Etching: a technique of print making in which the plate is covered with a waxy substance, and the design scratched onto it with an etching needle, exposing the metal beneath. Acid will thus only bite into the lines, which will subsequently hold the ink.

Foxing: the brown spots of mould which will attack a paper which has been allowed to get damp. Removal is usually an easy job for a restorer.

Impression: the individual print; also used as an indication of its place in an edition as in 'an early impression of the first state'.

Laid Down: stuck to a backing paper or board. (Be suspicious, this may well be an attempt to disguise damage and repairs.)

Limited Edition: modern prints should be numbered and the plates destroyed or defaced on completion. It is of course impossible to estimate the size of the editions of Old Master prints. The limit on some modern editions has run up to 1,000 or so. Be wary of these. Obviously, the larger the edition, the more worn the plates will become.

Lithograph: a process patented by a German, Aloys Senefelder, in 1801 which gradually replaced aquatint as the preferred method of producing topographical and sporting prints. An advantage is that the lines produced have very much of the feel of original pencil work. Basically, the drawing is made with a waxy lithographic crayon on a porous prepared stone, which is then soaked in water. Since the ink used, which is called *tusche*, also has a grease base, it will only adhere to the drawn lines. Colouring was once again done by hand. Modern derivatives, such as transfer lithography and photolithography, inhabit an ill-defined border region between original and reproduction.

Gerald Leslie Brockhurst: *Adolescence.* 1932. Etching, 37 × 26·5 cm.

The density of this image is quite remarkable for an etching, and the effect is very close to that of mezzotint.

Thomas Shotter Boys: *Oxford Circus*, from a set of 26 coloured tinted lithographs entitled *London as it is*, published in 1842. L. 32·2 × 44·5 cm.

Henri l'Evêque: *Vue de Genève prise des Eaux Vives.* c.1770. Coloured etching. P. 36·8 × 55·2 cm.

Prince Rupert: *The Great Executioner,* after Ibert. 1658. Mezzotint, 64 × 46 cm. Oxford, Ashmolean Museum.

Margin: the area of blank paper outside the image or platemark. It may be used for signatures or letterpress. As paper was expensive, the Old Masters tended to leave very narrow, or 'thread' margins, but with eighteenth-century and later examples you should often be wary of narrow margins, since they may have been cut to disguise damage.

Measurements: these are usually given height before width and in millimetres for accuracy, but do not be too disturbed if those of your example vary slightly from those given in a *catalogue raisonné*, since paper may contract or expand after printing. A good catalogue entry will make it plain whether the measurements refer to the size of the image, the platemark or the full margins. 'Sight' measurements require caution, because they probably mean that the cataloguer has not taken the print out of its frame.

Mezzotint: the mezzotint process is the reverse of most of the others, since the artist works from a black ground to a lighter design. The whole surface of the plate is first roughened with a rouleau or a rocker, so that it is all burr, and then polished and smoothed down to produce the design. This means that it relies on shade and tone rather than outline for its effect, and makes it particularly suitable for the reproduction of oil paintings. It was invented by a German officer, Ludwig von Siegen, in the middle of the seventeenth-century, and he taught it to Prince Rupert of the Rhine, who brought it to England at the Restoration. It was much used for portrait prints over the next fifty years, but then went out of fashion until the second half of the eighteenth century. After a second vogue of about fifty years it again fell into disuse, but it has been revived once more in recent decades by a number of excellent artists, such as Giorgio Morandi.

Mixed Media: the use of several different processes in one print.

Platemark: the impression left by the edge of a metal plate, which is usually slightly bevelled so as not to cut the paper.

Proof before Letters: a print which was pulled before the addition of the title or any other textual lettering.

Recto: the front face of a paper.

Remarque: a small drawing or additional print in the margin and separate from the main subject. It was a device used by late nineteenth-century engravers and etchers to designate a special edition. The *remarque* is often a comment on the main subject, and it should be accompanied by the signature of the artist and the printer if any.

Restrike: an unauthorized late edition printed from an original plate, perhaps many years after the death of the artist. Pierre François Basan, for instance, produced editions from at least seventy-nine Rembrandt plates at the end of the eighteenth century.

Screen Print: a common modern method employing a finely meshed screen, often of silk, and stencils to transfer the image to paper, rather than a plate or block.

Francis Bacon: *Triptych.* Etching and lithograph. Published 1981 in an edition of 99, each print signed and numbered. Image size, 39 × 93·5 cm.

Andy Warhol: *Marilyn.* 1971. Silk-screen print, 91·4 × 91·4 cm. London, Tate Gallery.

Joan Miró: *Colpir Sense Nafrar I*. Lithograph. Published 1981 in an edition of 50, each print signed and numbered. Image and paper size 96 × 72·5 cm.

Graham Bannister: *Imaginary View from the Artist's Studio*. Printed in 1983. Screenprint, image size 57 × 43 cm.

Henri de Toulouse-Lautrec: *Reine de Joie*. 1892. Coloured lithograph, 136 × 91 cm.

Soft-ground Etching: a technique in which the plate is coated with a soft substance such as beeswax, and the drawing made on a paper placed on top. The coating will adhere to the paper where lines have been made, thus exposing the metal to be bitten by acid. These lines will then hold ink as in a normal etching.

State: on no account to be confused with 'impression' or 'edition'. In between the various states of a particular plate the artist may make alterations, additions and corrections. This can happen several times before the plate is worn out; many Rembrandt prints, for example, exist in six or so states. Thus you should not assume that a first state is automatically more desirable than a third or a sixth. In this context, last thoughts may be best, and other factors can affect value. For example, only two impressions of a certain state might be known, which could make them more valuable in academic and market terms than a more common if more aesthetically satisfying earlier or later state.

Rembrandt Harmensz. van Rijn, *Christ Healing the Sick* ('The Hundred Guilder Print'). Etching with drypoint and burin, second state (of three), a very good impression, still with considerable burr . . . generally in excellent, fresh condition. P. 28 × 38·6 cm. Sold 17 June 1981 for £17,000.

Second state, a fair impression underinked in places . . . several nicks and small losses in the thread margins, two repairs on the left-hand side and other minor damage, slight foxing. Sold 13 May 1969 for £1,450.

Second state, a later impression of this state . . . with margins (partly missing at the lower left corner), a small surface loss at the lower right corner, two pinholes towards the top (three or more in the margins), the platemark weak in places, some stains and creases. Sold 3 November 1981 for £1,400.

Stipple Engraving: a pointillist manner of engraving which was much favoured by Francesco Bartolozzi (1725–1815) and the engravers of the late eighteenth century. It can have a soft, pencil-like effect, a little like lithography, which superseded it.

Trimmed: a term indicating that a print has been cut down from its original margins to the platemark, or to the subject, or to wherever is specified. Except where it has been done deliberately by an artist such as James Abbott McNeill Whistler (1834–1903), this is not desirable – but it might gain you a good print which you could not afford in pristine condition.

Verso: the reverse of a sheet of paper.

Wood Cut: a print making technique in which the block is cut away to leave the design in relief, rather than incised as in a wood engraving. The same is true of humbler forms of printmaking such as the lino cut, or even the potato cut.

With this terminology in mind, let us look at a couple of typical catalogue entries for prints.

REMBRANDT HARMENSZ. van RIJN

ABRAHAM'S SACRIFICE (B., Holl. 35; H. 283; BB. 55-E)

etching with drypoint, a fine impression, with considerable burr, printed with a light tone and delicate wiping marks, with small margins, slight foxmarks, generally in very good condition, laid at three corners
P. 156 × 131mm.

PROVENANCE: T. J. Thompson (L. 2442)

after HENRY ALKEN

THE QUORN HUNT, by F. C. Lewis (S. p.62)

coloured aquatints, the set of eight, fairly good impressions, published by R. Ackermann, London, 1835, trimmed on or just inside the platemark, some slight staining and spotting, generally in good condition, laid, framed
S. 430 × 605mm   (8)

In the first case the print is definitely a Rembrandt, so the full name of the artist is given. The letters and figures in brackets after the title refer to the several *catalogues raisonnés* of his printed work (Bartsch, Holstein, Hind and Biorklund Barnard). It is basically an etching, but some details have been added with the drypoint. It appears to be an early impression, because of the burr; the wiping marks, made when cleaning surplus ink from the plate just before printing, give a personal touch. The margins are small, as you would expect with a seventeenth-century print, but they have not been trimmed subsequently. The slight foxing is no problem, but it should be attended to immediately to prevent it spreading. The fact that it is laid at only three of the corners means that you can have a look at the

(*Above left*) Rembrandt Harmensz. van Rijn: *St. Jerome Reading in an Italian Landscape*. Etching, drypoint and engraving, *c*.1653. First state (of two), a magnificent impression . . . printed with some tone and charged with burr. P. 25·8 × 20·5 cm. Sold 1 November 1983 for £122,835.

(*Centre*) First state, a very fine impression on Japan paper. Sold 24 November 1970 for £12,000.

(*Right*) Second state, engraving and drypoint, a fine impression with some burr, generally in good condition. Sold 2 July 1975 for £2,625.

back if you are careful. If you buy it you should have it removed from the old backing paper – for heaven's sake do not try to do this yourself, however simple a job it looks – and remounted on acid-free modern Museum Board. The 'P' indicates that the measurements are those of the platemark. The print was once in the collection of T. J. Thompson, who was active in the first half of the nineteenth century, and carries his collector's mark. You will find this discussed in Fritz Lugt's *Les Marques de Collections de Dessins et d'Estampes* (1921 and 1956), as number 2442.

The second example takes us to a very different taste and market, that for English hunting prints. This is an example of one of the most desirable of such sets. Just as there is an order of social primacy among the hunts themselves, so is there in the prints depicting them. 'S. p.62' here refers

Albrecht Dürer: Apocalypse: *St. Michael Fighting against the Dragon*. 1498. Woodcut, 29·4 × 23·3 cm.

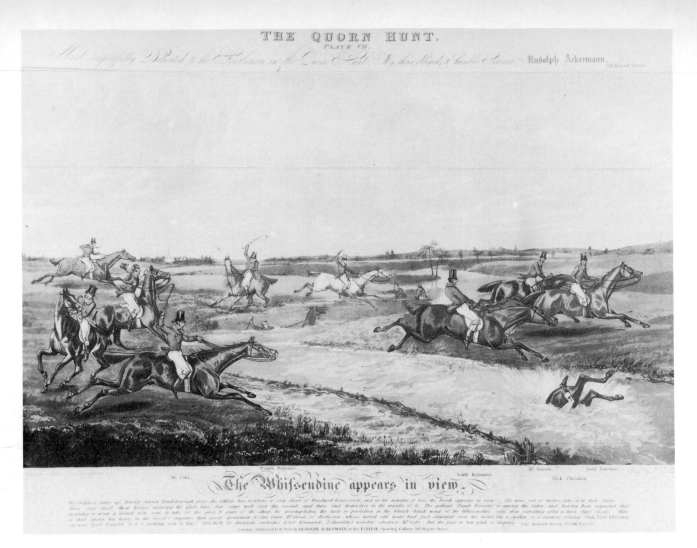

THE QUORN HUNT.
PLATE VII.

Most respectfully Dedicated to the Gentlemen in the Quorn Hunt, By their Obliged & humble Servant, Rudolph Ackermann, 191 Regent Street.

The Whissendine appears in view.

not to a *catalogue raisonné* but to Siltzer's *The Story of British Sporting Prints*, page 62, a work that is long out of print but can be consulted at any good reference library. The original paintings or watercolours here were by Henry Alken, one of the leading artists in this field, and the printmaker was Frederick Christian Lewis, who was the father of J. F. Lewis, R.A., and a considerable artist in his own right. Rudolph Ackermann was one of the leading publishers of such things. Unfortunately this set has lost its margins, which will lower the value, but otherwise it appears to be in good condition, although take a careful look for repairs because of that warning 'laid'. The measurement designation 'S' could lead to confusion, since it could mean subject, sight or sheet, and this is nowhere indicated in the catalogue. In this case it means sheet, and the measurements must be an average, because of the trimming. If you are just looking for good quality decoration, then this set could be an admirable buy. If you want the best, then pass it up and await a better opportunity.

The first thing that must be done by anyone contemplating buying a print is to look at it out of its frame. Only thus can you be sure that it is all that it is claimed to be. Hold it up to the light and examine the paper. Does

After Henry Alken: *The Quorn Hunt*, the set of eight plates, by F. C. Lewis. Coloured aquatints, part of a J. Whatman watermark, good, uniform, early impressions, published by R. Ackermann, February 1835, trimmed on the platemark . . . generally in good condition with some slight staining and foxing.

This is one of the most sought-after sets of English sporting prints, but condition can greatly affect price. While by no means perfect this one sold for £2,800 in 1978. The previous year a very similar but much more damaged set had reached only £480.

it appear to be the right age? Are there any distinguishing features? The history of papermaking is too vast a subject to be tackled here, but you should be aware of the salient characteristics of papers of different dates, and Dard Hunter's *Papermaking* (1967) provides an excellent introduction to the subject.

Next you should look for a watermark. This feature arrived early as a natural development of the paper-making process, since paper was made on wire frames or moulds on which fibrous pulp made from rags was shaken to form sheets. As the pulp dried the lines of the wires would remain as lighter stripes which showed when the sheet was held to the light. It did not take long for the makers to include individual patterns in the mould to show where the sheet had been made. One of the earliest, which was used by Dürer but also in much later papers, was a rudimentary ox-head. Others derived from the arms of the city of manufacture, as in the case of Augsburg or of the Strasburg 'bend and lily'. Such marks, however, cannot be taken as proof of place of origin since they were adopted by makers in quite different cities and countries and seem to have been used to denote sheet size. As a result of a tax law, British paper is quite often dated from 1794, and it may also carry an excise number from which the mill of origin may be deduced. However

Rembrandt van Rijn: *The Angel Departing from the Family of Tobias.* Etching and drypoint, Hollstein's first state (of four), a very fine impression carefully printed with excellent contrasts, especially noticeable in the central group, with considerable burr on all the drypoint work.

This particularly good and early impression sold for £5,500 in 1976. The same sale also included a second state which made £1,600 and a third state which made £1,100.

dating was not necessary after 1811, although often still used, and the excise system was abandoned in 1851. Thus a watermark will not necessarily date something exactly for you, but it may help to establish the general period.

Much less welcome is the presence of lines of light around the plate-mark since these may indicate that the original margins were damaged and have been cut away. The subject has then been let into new margins. If you are a purist this may spoil the print for you.

At this point try to assess whether the print has full margins or has been trimmed, and look out for any repairs to the paper. You may even find that some of the lines have been filled in or strengthened by hand with a pen. All these factors should lower the price.

Collectors' marks will be discussed in connection with Old Master drawings (p. 133), but they are even more commonly found on prints. You must get to know your predecessors in the field and remember which of them add stature, and which are less desirable. Even the mark of a great museum collection, such as the Albertina in Vienna, may not be a cause of outright rejoicing: the museum may have had two impressions and sold off the less satisfactory one. On the other hand, a good provenance can add immensely to the pleasure of ownership.

One of the great advantages that the collector of prints has is that almost every important print has been catalogued, and almost every major artist has been accorded the accolade of a *catalogue raisonné*. These will not only record states and sizes, but also any copies or restrikes that are known, so if you do your homework before buying, there is little excuse for ending up with a dud. In fact, it is rarely worth a forger's time to make new plates and exact copies of Old Master prints, since the process is very laborious, and the costs must be almost as high as buying an original. An exception in recent years has been a group of 'Piranesi' etchings which are remarkably difficult to tell from the originals. Every line and blemish seems to be there. Presumably these were financially worth the effort, since a fine print maker devoted a great deal of time to them. As with Old Master drawings, you are much more likely to come across dangerously good modern mechanical reproductions and photocopies.

If I had to recommend an area which was still underpriced, and in which a splendid and comprehensive collection might still be formed, I would point to the mezzotint. With the exceptions of the greatest examples – Prince Rupert's *Great Executioner*, Richard Earlom's (1743–1822) *Fruit Piece* and *Flower Piece* after Jan van Huysum, and a few by Earlom and others after paintings by Joseph Wright of Derby (1734–97) – the price of mezzotints rarely reflects their artistic value. Another possibility is British twentieth-century etching. Although prices have risen markedly over the last decade or so, even the best examples have yet to reach the levels of the 1920s. I have bought excellent eighteenth-century mezzotints for £5 or less during the last ten years, and good twentieth-century etchings by some of the best artists for less than £10. Yet another area in which there has been renewed interest, but there is still a considerable amount of meat on the bone, is late eighteenth- and early nineteenth-century caricature prints. Here one might point to

Richard Earlom after Jan van Huysum: *Fruit Piece*. 1723. Mezzotint.

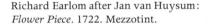

Richard Earlom after Jan van Huysum: *Flower Piece*. 1722. Mezzotint.

Thomas Rowlandson: *The Boxes*. Published 12 December 1809. Hand-coloured etching.

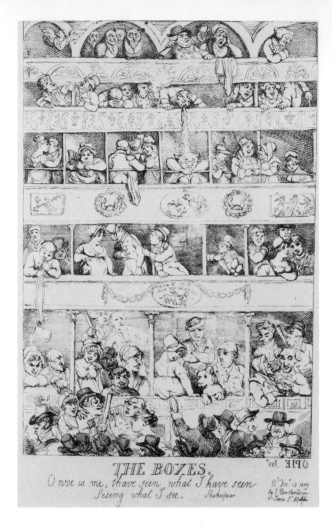

Thomas Rowlandson (1756–1827), James Gillray (1757–1815), and even to Honoré Daumier (1808–79).

Prints made by American artists in the eighteenth and early nineteenth century are mainly collected for their historical interest. American prints considered as fine art begin with the work of John James Audubon (1785–1851). The 435 prints in his massive work *The Birds of America* (1827–38) are among the most sought after and expensive by any American artist, and are staples of the sale room. Prints from paintings by George Caleb Bingham (1811–79) share some of the popularity of his paintings.

The lithographs issued by the firm of Currier & Ives, New York City, from 1857 to 1906, of which nearly 7,000 subjects (landscapes, marine, portraits, etc.) have been identified, are perennially popular with American collectors. One advantage for the beginner is that they sell over an unusually wide range of price, depending on rarity and subject.

Among the major American printmakers of the late nineteenth century, the most important in today's estimation was Winslow Homer

FASHION *before* EASE;

or, — *A good Constitution sacrificed for a Fantastick Form*.

ULYSSE ET PENELOPE.

(1836–1910), whose work began with his wood engravings of the Civil War. Another important figure within the U.S. and in Paris was Mary Cassatt (1844–1926), whose prints in the Impressionist vein are now among the most expensive modern prints. Entire sales of her graphic work have been held in recent years. The reputation of James Abbott McNeill Whistler has risen and fallen, but at the moment his etchings and lithographs are again widely collected.

Since the Second World War print making in the U.S. has taken on new life. Artists, including those of the New York School of the 1950s to 1970s, have turned from painting to printmaking, and many single prints, series, and portfolios of their work have been issued. The market is extremely active, and the prints appear not only at dealers' galleries but also constantly at auction. Important names include Alexander Calder (1898–1976), Jim Dine (b. 1935), Robert Indiana (b. 1928), Robert Rauschenberg (b. 1925), and, especially, Jasper Johns (b. 1930). Collecting their graphic work is widespread not only in the U.S., but also in Europe, especially in Germany and Switzerland, and in Japan. This is also true of other living artists who have built up an international reputation, such as Salvador Dali (b. 1904), Henry Moore (b. 1898) and, from the younger generation, David Hockney (b. 1937).

(*Left*) James Gillray: *Fashion before Ease; or, – A Good Constitution Sacrificed, for a Fantastick Form*. Published 2 January 1793. Hand-coloured etching, 31·8 × 24·1 cm.

(*Above*) Honoré Daumier: *Ulysses and Penelope*. Lithograph published in *Charivari*, 26 June 1842. From the series *Histoire Ancienne*.

View of New York from Brooklyn Heights.
Lithograph published by N. Currier in
1849.

David Hockney: *The Hypnotist*. 1963.
Etching and aquatint, printed in two
colours, 50·2 × 50 cm.

5. Watercolours and Drawings

Although nowadays we tend to think of watercolours as a type of painting, this is only a comparatively recent categorization. Originally they were only regarded as coloured line drawings, rather than as formal finished works of art in their own right. This sometimes logical division is still maintained by many salerooms and connoisseurs, although there is often now an immense financial gulf between the charcoal or pastel sketches of, say, a Corot or a Degas – who, incidentally, was originally spelt De Gas – and the full watercolour paintings of even the greatest practitioners. With regard to the drawings and doodles of the major nineteenth-century artists we need say little, since for the most part we cannot afford them. However, because of inherited prejudice, a consummate watercolour could still be within the reach of even a collector on a limited budget, while an undistinguished 'drawing' in the modern sense might not. This is partly a matter of date. Since the end of the last century even charcoal has been rendered less fugitive. Eighteenth-century pastel portraits are splendid when they happen to have survived in good condition. Late nineteenth-century and twentieth-century pastels are likely to survive in good condition, and their relative prices reflect this.

The term 'watercolour' and 'amateurish' have often been taken as synonyms by the mocking and the ignorant. For them the whole phenomenon is encapsulated by the image of groups of maiden ladies sketching when the weather permitted. It is true that the medium has always attracted amateurs, and that the majority of the masters earned their livelihood as teachers, but such amateurs have by no means always been amateurish. In Britain, until well into the nineteenth century the most usual amateur was male, and perhaps military. From the middle of the eighteenth century, first-class drawing masters were attached to the military academies, and an ability to make an accurate record in watercolour, or at least in pencil, was regarded as an essential skill for the naval or army officer. Many of these men took a taste for the art back into civilian life and passed it on to their families and friends, often summoning their old masters to teach the new devotees.

As often as not the division between the amateur and the professional was one of class rather than pure ability, and it was not until com-

Jean Baptiste Camille Corot: *Paysage.*
*c.*1870–2(?). Soft pencil on paper,
12·5 × 19·5 cm.

paratively late in the nineteenth century that a gentleman could turn professional without attracting some stigma. All this has an advantage, as well as a drawback, for the collector. There are many more competent watercolours about than could ever have been produced by the professional watercolour painters, and thus it is still possible to collect good things without unacceptable expense, but at the same time the problems of attribution are increased. It is easy to forget that many of the masters were very good teachers indeed and to attribute anything to them that is in their style and not clearly signed by someone else. Many good amateurs rarely signed, and in the course of time their work may quite innocently be credited to a better-known professional – sometimes to the detriment of his overall reputation.

In some ways the choices open to the collector of watercolours are greater than those available to someone in search of oil paintings. Exigency of space is less limiting, and a group of portraits in watercolour, for instance, can be displayed in less formal surroundings and with less crushing effect than a similar collection of oil paintings. The same is true of marine subjects, and even the grander landscapes. It is also a more practical field in which to build up a theme collection, whether by place or by type of artist. Here the 'distinguished amateurs', as they were dubbed by Iolo Williams, provide many opportunities. You might, perhaps, concentrate on early women watercolourists, eighteenth-century clergy-men, naval officers or aristocrats. One of the most interesting private collections in London takes the Near and Middle East as its theme. It was built up in the days before orientalist subjects became popular and expensive, and now it is a major source of information for academics studying Middle Eastern topics, as well as for watercolour collectors.

It is almost inevitable that any book on collecting will have occasional 'you should have been here yesterday' passages. Here is mine. The great days for the collector of English watercolours were the years from the end

Harry John Johnson: *Hampstead*.
From an album of watercolours,
36·2 × 31·8 cm. overall.

Edward Duncan: *Sheep Washing*.
Pencil, pen and brown ink. From an
album of agricultural sketches,
18·1 × 22·9 cm. maximum.

William Leighton Leitch. *Rome: A
Church Tower among the Roofs*. Inscribed
and dated 1 January 1855. Watercolour
heightened with white, 21·9 × 33·9 cm.

A number of nineteenth- and twentieth-
century artists used studio stamps
instead of signatures. Such a stamp may
also indicate that the drawing was part of
the studio sale after the artist's death.
Many of them are listed with collectors'
marks in Lugt.

Eugène Boudin: *Sur la Plage*. 1869.
Signed lower right 'E. Boudin' and
numbered in pencil '69'. Watercolour
and pencil on paper, 15 × 26·5 cm.

The studio stamp of the artist
Myles Birket Foster.

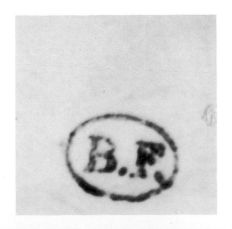

of the Second World War to the early 1960s. Very few people were interested or knew what to look for, and the few connoisseurs such as Iolo Williams, Professor J. Isaacs, L. G. Duke and Martin Hardie could pick up wonderful things by the bundle in the old book and print shops of Bloomsbury and the Charing Cross Road. These men and their friends and rivals have now passed into the history of the subject, and the modern collector should take particular note of items which mention them in the provenance. Some earlier collectors used collectors' marks, and these will be found in Fritz Lugt's great compendium. While the mark of a good collection is obviously an excellent thing to find on a drawing or watercolour, you must not let yourself be carried away by it. The initials of William Esdaile, for instance, are often found on Gainsborough drawings, but Esdaile also possessed a number of examples by Gainsborough's friend and imitator George Frost of Ipswich.

The new collector of watercolours – like the new collector of any of the other sorts of picture mentioned in this book – will need to familiarize himself with the terms used by artists and dealers: a watercolour is a work, for the most part on paper, which employs translucent colours so that light is reflected not only from the paint surface, but also from that of the paper beneath. Albrecht Dürer was probably the first major European artist to use it, in a series of landscape studies, but for most critics it was brought to perfection as a branch of painting in its own right in England during the eighteenth and early nineteenth centuries. In the twentieth century many of the greatest artists in Britain and in the rest of Europe and the United States have used the medium with distinction, but it is no longer so relevant to think of 'watercolour artists' as opposed to 'oil painters'. For the most part, as far as artists themselves are concerned, the boundaries between media are very much less important than they used to be.

Works in gouache, bodycolour or poster paint are often lumped together with watercolours, but in essence they are quite different, since bodycolour, like oil paint, is opaque. When touches of bodycolour, usually white, are added to a watercolour, the technique is referred to as

'heightening'. This term can also be used of gum arabic. This is an acacia resin which is used to bind watercolours to each other and the paper, but further gum is sometimes added, giving an effect like a varnished oil painting.

Monochrome wash drawings can also be taken under the heading of watercolours. Here a wash of brown, grey or perhaps blue is used to give form and depth to a line drawing, and the local colours are left to the imagination. Eighteenth- and nineteenth-century examples are well

Giorgio Morandi: *Natura morta*. Signed lower left. Watercolour on paper, 22 × 33 cm.

Myles Birket Foster: *The Unruly Donkey*. Pencil and watercolour, heightened with white, 26·7 × 41·2 cm.

worth looking out for, as are pencil drawings, because they are often much cheaper than fully coloured works.

As with any other work on paper, you should always try to see a watercolour out of its frame, if it has one, before deciding to buy it. There are often signatures and inscriptions on the reverse, and both paper and paint can tell you much about its age. If it is in an old frame, it will almost certainly need to be re-mounted, because old mounts can cause staining and foxing. The new mount should be made of Museum or Conservation Board, which are acid-free. Fashions in framing and mounting change, and

Myles Birket Foster: *The Watering-Place.* Signed with monogram. Pencil, watercolour and bodycolour, 77·4 × 67·5 cm.

(*Above, left*) William Henry Hunt: *Light and Shade*. Signed and dated 1835. Watercolour with gum arabic, 32·4 × 24·4 cm.

This watercolour has suffered in the long run from too great a use of gum arabic. The surface has cracked and roughened in some places.

(*Above, right*) William Henry Hunt: *Black Grapes in a Basket*. Watercolour, 20·3 × 25·4 cm.

A good illustration of the pointilliste technique used by a number of nineteenth-century watercolourists including Hunt and Foster.

John White Abbott: *On the Dart from Holme Chase, Devon*. Inscribed and dated 16 July 1800. Pen and grey ink and watercolour, 17·5 × 24·1 cm.

White Abbott almost always inscribed on the reverse. It should be automatic practice to take a drawing or watercolour out of its frame.

J. Lory: *A Distant View of the Matterhorn*. Pencil and watercolour, 19·2 × 27·5 cm.

The Lory family produced many prints of Swiss scenery. Their drawings are well worth seeking out.

currently the simple approach, with perhaps a wash line or two on the mount, is in vogue. However, it is best not to be too slavish about this, since some Victorian examples are still most at home in their original sombre gold, and others can be set off admirably by a mount in a sympathetic colour.

An important thing to remember when trying to identify an early English or European watercolour is that many of the landscapes and topographical subjects, even by amateurs, were used for book illustrations and prints. If you can identify the subject you may be able to work backwards to the artist by way of the topographical and picturesque publications of the period. If you know the artist but not the subject, find out what publications he produced or contributed to. In the 1820s and 1830s there was a great vogue for 'Annuals', such as *The Landscape Annual* and *The Copper-Plate Annual*, which contained literary illustrations as well as landscapes and antiquities. In some cases the subject will virtually tell you the artist. An eighteenth-century bodycolour view of Richmond in Yorkshire, especially on quite a large scale, is likely to be by George Cuit (1743–1818), and a mid-nineteenth-century view of Dover or its castle could well be by William Burgess (1805–61).

Do not be put off by something which appears to be in poor condition,

sometimes a great deal of faded colouring can be retrieved by a gentle clean. A coating of mould can be a positive advantage, since it is likely to put off other bidders, and it is easy to remove yourself. Take the drawing out of its frame and keep it in a dry place with an even temperature – but not too hot – for about a week and then simply brush the mould away. If you have any doubts, consult a restorer before buying. It is sensible to learn a little about the history of pigments and paper-making, since these will help you to estimate date as well as condition. For instance, Chinese White was only introduced to England in 1834, before which opaque whites were little used on watercolours – and they have often oxidized. In some cases fading cannot be reversed, notably in the skies of Peter de Wint (1784–1849), which are often pink if they have survived at all. This is because many machine-made papers in the first half of the nineteenth century contained too much acid, and this attacked blues in particular. When looking at a faded example, always look at the edges which have been covered by a mount. Here the colours may have retained their original strength, and they can give you an idea of how it could look when restored.

Since the 1960s the prices for most types of watercolour have risen dramatically. The best English examples are now often quite as expensive as oil paintings, although this does not mean that the whole field is out of the reach of all but the very rich. However, there is a temptation to accept things of lesser quality, and this should be strongly resisted. Never buy a

Winslow Homer: *Sponge Boats, Key West*. Signed and dated 1903. Watercolour and pencil on paper, 35·5 × 55·5 cm.

This painting was sold for £350,000 on 3 November 1982 – a record auction price for an American watercolour, and for a work by Homer (see page 99).

Peter de Wint: *Landscape*. Watercolour, 28·6 × 45·7 cm.

Thomas Shotter Boys: *Le Pont Royal, Paris. c.*1827(?). Watercolour, 32 × 52·7 cm.

Joseph Bolegard: Design for 'Vogue'.
Signed and dated lower right 'J.B.22'.
Watercolour and pencil on paper,
33·5 × 27 cm.

second-rate thing by an important artist merely for the name. You will do much better to concentrate on the best examples of less well-known painters.

Because of the remarkable way in which the English school developed, it can be worth keeping a look out for examples of other eighteenth-century European schools. If, for instance, you can find a good French or Dutch watercolour of the period off its home territory, it is likely to be less expensive than the English equivalent. Currently, in fact, the English eighteenth century, too, could be said to be undervalued against later work.

Early American watercolours are complicated by the fact that prices can be determined by rarity and subject as well as quality. Watercolours of the early nineteenth century, both portraits and landscapes, are avidly collected. Without regard to their artistic merit, many of these have

Albert Namatjira: *Ranges near Mount Gillen*. Signed, and signed and inscribed on the reverse. Watercolour, 25·4 × 35·6 cm.

Ernst Ludwig Kirchner: *Streetscene*. Signed and dated 12. Pen, black ink, brush and grey wash, 51 × 38 cm.

George Grosz: *Das Paar. c.*1917(?) Signed lower right. Watercolour on paper, 57·5 × 46 cm.

Joseph Mallord William Turner:
*Cologne from the River with Figures
Bathing from Boats in the Foreground.*
*c.*1817(?) Signed twice. Watercolour,
24·1 × 33 cm.

considerable historical importance since the American West was first painted by artists in watercolour. Among the most notable artists of this period are Karl Bodmer (1809–93) and Alfred Jacob Miller (1810–74), both of whom visited the unexplored West in the 1830s. They established a tradition of painting Western scenes in watercolour that has persisted into the twentieth century and includes painters such as Charles Marion Russell (1864–1926), who worked primarily in watercolour, and Frederic Remington (1861–1909).

The major American nineteenth-century watercolourist was Winslow Homer (1836–1910), whose works in that medium – usually landscapes of Maine or the West Indies or marine subjects – are among the most expensive American watercolours today.

Among twentieth-century artists, the watercolours of Charles Demuth

(1883–1935), who worked almost exclusively in the medium, painting flowers, still lifes, and circus scenes, are highly esteemed, as are those of Maurice Prendergast (1861–1924), John Marin (1870–1953), and Reginald Marsh (1889–1954).

Among living artists Andrew Wyeth (b. 1917) is one of the best known practitioners, and important works by him have entered collections not only in the U.S. but on the Continent and Japan. The tradition survives even into Pop Art and beyond.

There is another field which could be exploited with profit by the collector, and that is the earlier English pen or wash drawing. Many of these seventeenth- and early eighteenth-century works inhabit an ill-defined border region between Old Master drawings and full water-colours, and it is an area which can be overlooked by the purists of the two specialities. In the same way French and Dutch eighteenth-century watercolourists are often overlooked outside their homelands. The works of Victor Jean Nicolle (1754–1826), for instance, can be very decorative, and would grace any collection.

Thomas Wakeman: *Battle Monument, Baltimore, USA*. Signed and inscribed. Watercolour, 52·1 × 75·5 cm.

Thomas Monro: *A Landscape Composition with a Cart. c.*1790(?) Black ink and wash, 17·9 × 15·9 cm.

Monro is much more important as a patron than as an artist, where he tended to follow Gainsborough. He used charcoal and little colour, which keeps his price low.

(*Below*) Edward William Cooke: *Palms in the Consul's Garden, Alicant.* 1860. Pencil, 21·9 × 33·7 cm. Private Collection.

Cooke was a fine painter and a splendid draughtsman. He also kept meticulous records of his works and travels. A drawing like this gives great pleasure, but costs much less than something coloured.

(*Above*) Walter Langley: *Sad News*. Signed and dated '85. Watercolour, 31·8 × 16·8 cm.

Pictures by an American artist will generally be much more expensive than similar work by a Briton of equivalent talent. Eakins's *Spinning* sold at auction in New York in 1983 for $550,000 (£343,750), while *Sad News*, by the British artist Walter Langley, sold for just £480 at Christie's in London in 1978.

(*Above*) Thomas Cowperthwait Eakins: *Spinning*. Signed and dated 1881. Watercolour on paper, 39·8 × 27 cm.

Robert Frederick Blum: *Geisha at her Toilet*. Stamped with artist's stamp. Pastel on paper laid on board, 36 × 29·5 cm.

6. Oil Paintings

The subject of oil paintings is in one way too vast, and in another too small, for much to be said about it in a specialist section. In terms of time, styles, schools, media, social and art history it is enormous, but at the same time most of the specific points which should be borne in mind by the would-be buyer will be found running through the other chapters of this book. An immense literature on almost every aspect of painting has been produced over the centuries, and it will be added to and revised as long as man and art exist.

The language used to describe paintings can be confusing, even impenetrable, for the beginner, so here is a brief list of some that may be encountered, together with notes on the more usual media and techniques. Naturally enough, many of the terms used for Old Masters are taken from the Italian and the French.

Acrylic: synthetic resin colours which have been produced since the 1950s and 1960s. The pigments are pre-mixed with an acrylic emulsion which takes the place of oil or egg in other media. Some pigments, such as Alizarin Crimson, cannot be used with acrylic.

Autoritratto: Italian for self-portrait.

Bloom: an opaque, cataract-like film which may form on an oil painting. In its early, bluish stage it can be polished off with a silk rag or a soft leather, or, since it is caused by damp, it can be dried out in sunlight. At later stages the picture may have to be revarnished.

Canvas: the 'cloath' ground used by early painters. It came into general use in the seventeenth century. It is generally made from flax, hemp, jute or cotton, and during the early nineteenth century a smooth canvas with a diagonal or twill weave was much favoured, especially for portraits. Modern canvases are often ready primed for painting. Before 1784 eighteenth-century British canvas bore a government stamp.

Cenacolo: Italian term for a painting of the Last Supper.

Conversation-piece: a less than life-size group portrait, with the sitters placed informally, as if in conversation.

Michael Ayrton: *Large Shore*. Signed and dated lower left *Michael Ayrton 59–60*. Acrylic on board, 74·3 × 125·7 cm.

Cassone: an Italian marriage-chest. The front panel, often richly decorated, is frequently treated as a work of art in its own right.

Chiaroscuro: literally the contrasting of light and shade. It is sometimes used of a monochrome or grisaille painting.

Copper: a painting ground used at many times, but particularly in the seventeenth century and for small-scale works. In the following century Latin American painters favoured it since it withstood both the climate and the attentions of bugs.

Cradling: a method of remedying cracks and warping in panels by attaching supports to the reverse. Variations are parqueting and grating.

Craquelure: the small surface cracks in the varnish of a painting.

Crépuscule: a twilight scene.

Diptych: a painting in the form of two hinged leaves. A triptych has three leaves, and a polyptych more. Many were painted as altarpieces.

Discolouration: it is an unlikely fact that oil paintings which are stored in darkened rooms face to the wall are more subject to discolouration than those which are exposed to light and air.

Easel picture: a small and portable painting, also called a cabinet picture. (The word easel, by the way, comes from the Dutch, *ezel*, a donkey.)

Fête Champêtre: a rustic festival. In Dutch and Flemish works this is known as a *kermesse*.

Fête Galante: an elegant revelry in the manner of Boucher or Watteau.

Genre: used to describe a painting of domestic life, or with humorous or anecdotal content.

Gesso: plaster of Paris mixed with glue or size to prime a surface before painting.

Half-length: descriptions of portraits – half-, three-quarter, full-length, and so on – which seem straightforward, can in fact be confusing, since the terms were also used in the eighteenth century to denote sizes of canvas. Thus a head and shoulders could still be described as a half-length in this sense.

Impasto: thick painting, usually in the lighter passages. It is roughly equivalent to white heightening in watercolour.

Kit-cat: either an almost three-quarter length portrait, or a canvas measuring 36 × 28 in. (91 × 71 cm.), on which such portraits were usually painted. The name comes from an eighteenth-century club, whose members were so painted.

Landskip: the seventeenth- and eighteenth-century English rendering of the Dutch word which subsequently became 'landscape'.

Leather: a painting ground much used by Byzantine and Medieval painters.

Modello: a small-scale sketch giving an accurate idea of a proposed larger scheme.

Nocturne: a night-piece, which may or may not be a moonlight-piece.

Oil: although oil is mentioned as a medium as early as the eleventh century, it only came into common use in the fourteenth and fifteenth.

Panel from the Morelli cassone. 1472. Tempera, 40·6 × 137·1 cm. London, Courtauld Gallery.

One of a pair of *cassoni* made on the occasion of a wedding between two Florentine families, the Morelli and the Nerli.

By the seventeenth century it had superseded tempera almost entirely. Its function is to bind the pigments to each other and to the ground. Many oils have been used, but the most popular has always been linseed − except in France, where artists preferred poppy. While the latter cracks easily, it is not so prone to yellowing with age.

Panels: most of the European paintings which survive from before the seventeenth century are painted on wood, and wood has often been used since in preference to canvas. Poplar was much used in Italy, and oak north of the Alps. Venetian paintings are often on fir from the Adige, and other favourites have been American cottonwood, ash, beech, chestnut, lime (particularly by tempera painters), mahogany, walnut and willow.

Pastiche or *pasticcio:* a painting by one artist in the manner of another.

Pentimento: a second thought or correction. With time this may rise like a ghost through the overpainting.

Pietà: the Virgin weeping over the dead Christ. When the body is held on the knees of the seated Virgin, the German term is *Vesperbild.*

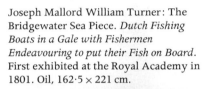

Joseph Mallord William Turner: The Bridgewater Sea Piece. *Dutch Fishing Boats in a Gale with Fishermen Endeavouring to put their Fish on Board.* First exhibited at the Royal Academy in 1801. Oil, 162·5 × 221 cm.

Plein Air: used of a painting executed out of doors. The term became a badge of the French, British and American landscape painters of the late nineteenth century, such as the Barbizon and Newlyn Schools.

Rissole: a French term for a painting with a golden quality of tone, such as many of the canvases of Rembrandt.

Tempera: painting with pigments ground in egg or in an emulsion. This was the most usual European medium until the late Middle Ages. It was revived in the United States during the first half of the nineteenth century, and has returned to universal popularity in the twentieth. A great advantage is that a properly prepared and finished tempera painting on wood is much less destructible than one in oil on canvas.

Tondo: also *rondo,* a circular painting.

Topographical painting: a landscape in which accuracy is more important than imaginativeness – though it may still be highly artistic.

Vanitas: a large and elaborate still life which may include a skull, documents and other mementoes of passing time.

Veduta: an Italian view of a city.

Vellum: many early miniatures, illuminations and drawings were on vellum, which is prepared calf-skin.

Vexierbild: a German term for a puzzle picture.

Circle of Jacob Savery II: *A Village Kermesse.* Dated 1625(?). Oil, 15·9 × 28 cm.

It is the ambition of every collector to wander into some dingy country sale room and there, in a corner, to light upon a gem disguised from all but the most discerning eye by layers of grime and coats of discoloured varnish. Unfortunately this is not only the ambition but also the livelihood of every good dealer too. As the auctioneers know, dealers may be tempted to bid more for a 'distressed' painting than one that has been recently restored, because their experience enables them to estimate the degree to which it can be reclaimed and the profit which could ensue. This is more difficult for the collector, unless he has taken the trouble to cultivate a good restorer, and to learn what is and what is not possible. In such circumstances there is rarely time to call up your restorer and to get him to have a look in person, so it would probably be unwise to take a gamble.

A useful aid here is a bottle of white spirit and a wad of cotton wool. A quick and gentle dab will not harm the painting, but it could give you a better idea of the true colours, and perhaps even disclose an unnoticed signature. However, this is a technique to be used surreptitiously. It is not likely to be encouraged by the sale room authorities, although they will probably have used it themselves, and you will not wish to be observed by any potential opposition, for fear of sharing the results. Luckily the white spirit will evaporate almost immediately, and the surface will return to dinginess.

In most cases dirt and discoloured varnish need not discourage you, since both can be removed without great difficulty. It is more difficult to assess the condition of the paint surface below. Experts differ as to the amount of repainting by a restorer that is legitimate. The situation is not as iniquitous as in the furniture business, where unscrupulous people have broken up one original chair and included the pieces in a newly made set of a dozen, describing the whole set as original. With paintings it is only possible to generalize. Some people, including leading dealers and eminent collectors, are happy even if as much as a third of the surface has been repainted. Others will not handle anything that has been more than patched and touched up, and yet others will allow a fair amount of repainting in, say, the sky, provided that the subject itself has not been tampered with.

So this is essentially a matter on which you must make up your own mind. One thing, however, you must consider when buying a distressed painting on canvas: it may very well have to be restretched and relined as well as cleaned. The stretcher is the wooden frame to which the canvas is attached, and this will often have warped, weakened or collapsed with age. It is a simple job to replace it, but an additional expense. Relining means sticking the original canvas onto a new one to back it. This will prevent any further movement which could make the paint surface crack and flake. Remember, if you do have a picture relined, you must be sure that the details of any old inscriptions or other information are transferred to the new backing. Check this with your restorer yourself, just in case he overlooks it. A Christie's stencil mark is likely to be on the stretcher. Obviously this cannot be transferred, but note it on a backing label. Naturally paintings on wood do not have these problems, but you may

(*Left and right*) Sir William Beechey: *Half-length Portrait of a Gentleman Writing*. Oil, 74 × 58 cm. Private Collection.

The illustrations show the painting before restoration, and halfway through the restoration process. In the partially restored state, where discoloured varnish has been removed, there are one or two areas of white plaster or gesso filling where repairs have been made previously. When the cleaning process has been completed, these areas will be restored.

have to have cracks and other damages attended to. In extreme cases it is possible to transfer the paint surface to a new panel: this is sometimes done with valuable icons, when one has been painted on top of another.

The ideal for the collector is to be able to build his collection at a time when the field is unfashionable, and then to watch other people fall into line and prices rise. This is a less practical ideal than it was in the past, because over the last thirty years almost everything has acquired its

admirers. Inevitably as one school, Impressionism, Surrealism or whatever, soars into the realms of financial impossibility, others, say High
Victorian or Post-Impressionism, must be found to cater for the demands
of the general ruck of collectors, and these in turn are boosted. This means
that tastes in collecting are probably more catholic than at any time before,
and also that there are more and more people ready to pounce on any
bargain or undervalued area that may present itself.

This can lead to the temptation to buy poor examples because nothing else seems to be available, and this should be strongly resisted. If you happen to like something that is unregarded for a reason other than lack of quality, then you should go for it, but do not expect the general taste to follow yours as a matter of course. For example, floral and fruity still lifes (never 'lives' by the way) have a ready and expensive sale, but similar things with dead game tend to have much less appeal. Certainly, they can spoil the appetites of the squeamish when hung in a dining-room. Thus buy fine examples by all means, but remember that if you should ever wish to re-sell, they are still likely to bring less than their softer and less gory equivalents.

Sir Edwin Landseer (1802–73) was immensely popular and successful in his own day, and totally disregarded for many years after his death. Now his technical and artistic merits are fully recognized once again, but much of his subject matter, whether gruesome, sentimental, or a mixture of both, still sticks in the craw of many potential collectors of Victorian paintings, and prices tend to be lower than his stature as an artist might warrant. In this case it is probably only a matter of time before quality overcomes any other doubts.

When looking for under-appreciated nineteenth-century painters, it is

Alfred Stannard: *Christmas Larder*. Signed and dated, 1856. Oil, 75 × 62·2 cm.

Flowers are always popular – corpses, particularly if well painted, are not always so.

Franz Xaver Petter:
*A Still life of
Tulips, Roses and
other Flowers in a
Vase on a Ledge.*
Signed. Oil,
80 × 59.6 cm.

worth studying the lists of what they exhibited and the prices which they charged during their careers. Allowing for the changing value of money, and the fact that much of the nineteenth century was a remarkably kind period to painters, it is easy enough to work out who is nowadays under-priced by comparison. Another point which must be remembered by the buyer of pictures of any period is the problem of school paintings, second versions and copies. Take, for instance, the small version of William Powell Frith's (1819–1909) *The Railway Station* (1862), which was offered by Sotheby's a few years ago. The auctioneers maintained that it was a second version painted by Frith himself, and estimated and publicized it accordingly. The art world disagreed, and a leading expert on Victorian painting, the dealer Jeremy Maas, unearthed virtually irrefutable proof that it was a perfectly legitimate copy by the less eminent Marcus Stone (1840–1921). Sotheby's stood by their guns and the picture was bought in, and if the price ever entered the sales indexes it doubtless did so as a poor result for a Frith, rather than as an outstanding one for a Stone.

Frans Post: *Brazilian Peasants Feasting and Merrymaking in a Village*. Signed and dated 164(or 5)3. Oil, 48 × 67·5 cm.

If Post had remained in Holland, he would not have stood out among the many second-rank landscape painters. However, he went to the then Dutch colony of Brazil, and this subject matter makes him a very expensive painter indeed.

Frederico Mazzotta: *Going to Market*.
Signed. Oil, 76·2 × 46·2 cm.

Mainstream nineteenth-century painters
– with obvious exceptions – do not often
have the international following of their
predecessors and successors. They tend
to be revered and collected in their
countries of origin, but to arouse little
interest elsewhere.

Petrus Van Schendel: *A Fishmarket at
Night*. Signed and dated 1847. Oil,
72 × 56·5 cm.
A great deal of nineteenth-century
mainstream painting derives from earlier
models. Naturally it should not be
dismissed on that account, providing
that it is technically accomplished.
Schendel may not have been particularly
original, but he was still good.

Theo van Rysselberghe: *Portrait de Jeune Fille*. Signed with monogram lower left. Oil, 46 × 38 cm.

Rudolf Ernst: *On the Steps of the Throne*. Signed. Oil, 71 × 91·5 cm.

Nineteenth-century 'Orientalist' works – paintings of Near and Middle-Eastern subjects by European artists – are now very expensive after decades of disdain.

John William Waterhouse: *Ophelia*.
Signed. Oil, 124·4 × 73·6 cm.

Changes in taste this century are
dramatically reflected in the
varying prices this painting has
reached at auction. It was sold for:
540 guineas in 1913, 20 guineas in
1950, 420 guineas in 1968, 3,000
guineas in 1971, £75,000 in 1982.

(*Above*) Anglo-Chinese School, *c*.1820: *A View of the Hongs at Canton*. Oil on brass, 11·4 × 15·2 cm.

The main collectors of views like this, which fall between the European and Chinese traditions, are those with far-Eastern connections. It will be interesting to see how this market will be affected in 1997 by the transfer of ownership of Hong Kong from the British to the Chinese.

(*Left*) George Grosz: *Stilleben mit Hampelmann*. Signed and dated on the reverse 'Grosz 27'. Oil, 63·5 × 50 cm.

Most people who set out to buy a Grosz would be looking for a biting satire in watercolour or pen and ink such as *Das Paar* (see page 98). However he could be a gentle painter, as in this still life.

Of course there are occasions when the faith of a buyer that he really has secured a great work under the guise of 'School of' or 'after' are fully justified, but almost always it is a long and frustrating task to prove it. The better known the painting the more difficult it is to unseat the previously accepted one, especially if the recognized version is in a great museum, since museums are very unhappy at losing face in such matters. A great collector is likely to take it at least as badly, since he will stand to lose money as well as face.

This sort of problem can arise quite frequently when dealing with portraits. A fashionable and successful portrait painter such as Sir Peter Lely (1618–80) or Sir Anthony van Dyck (1599–1641) would employ studio assistants on all but the most prestigious commissions, often doing no more than the face and hands himself. If the popularity of the sitter warranted it, as with King Charles I and his queen, Henrietta Maria, or if there were requests for copies from members of the sitters' families, then further copies would be made in the studio, and these might never be touched by the master's hand at all. In such cases quality must be the first

Cornelius Krieghoff: *An Indian Woman Wearing Snowshoes*. Signed. Oil, 26 × 21 cm.

Krieghoff's paintings can be technically crude, but the Canadian subject matter makes them expensive. This combination has naturally attracted forgers.

consideration, but it should be backed up by hard documentary evidence. Provenance is all important. If you can prove that your version has a straight pedigree back to the sitter or at least his family, while that in the National Portrait Gallery or wherever has no strong links, then you are part of the way there, but remember that in attribution, as in law, it is the claimant who must prove his case.

Oil sketches are a different matter and can provide many opportunities for the collector. Some artists made them as a matter of course in a regular progress from drawing to finished painting, others as independent memoranda for their own use. In either case they can have an extra fascination, since they show something of the workings of the artist's mind. Like working drawings they are a form of shorthand, and that is why they often have a more modern feel than fully finished paintings. This is particularly noticeable with that great sketcher John Constable, and even more dramatically in the work of his near contemporary the animal painter James Ward (1769–1859). In some of his sketches Ward

Antwerp School: *Fishwives at a Stall.* c.1620. Oil, 108 × 155 cm.

This is the sort of thing to which Schendel (p.115) was harking back.

James Ward: *John Levett Hunting in the Park at Wychnor*. 1817. Oil, 102 × 127 cm.

A fully finished painting by Ward. The action of the horses is natural, but it is still more lifelike in some of his impressionistic sketches.

was the first man to depict the correct action of a horse's legs in motion, many decades before other painters and the public became aware of it through photography. However in finished paintings he, too, stuck to the traditional, and unnatural, full-stretch posture.

Again, whatever one may feel about Landseer's usual subject matter, his small, free landscape sketches, often in the Highlands of Scotland, are glorious things which raise the heart. It might be possible to find one of these that is on the cheap side, because many people still tend to place an artist's whole work within a certain price-range, rather than looking at the merits of individual examples. Provided that you are convinced that what is untypical is right, rather than misattributed, you will often do very well to buy it. However, if you are concerned with an ultimate re-sale value, perhaps you should stick to what is instantly recognizable.

It is very difficult to point to any area or school which is now seriously undervalued – although it is not so hard so think of some that are distinctly over-priced. One in which good buys can still often be made is that of early portraits. English Tudor portraits and their equivalents elsewhere are often unattributable and their sitters impossible to identify. The only inscription is likely to be 'Aet. suae xxxj' or the like. If there is a coat-of-arms something might be done, but identification is still a very difficult task. This can put off buyers, as can the size of full-length examples, but they are often very decorative and considerable works of art.

Late nineteenth-century portraits will also bear consideration, provided that you only look for the ones which stand out as paintings. Many are dull, worthy and ultimately lifeless, and have little appeal unlesss they show members of your own family. A Sargent or a Winterhalter is a fine thing, whoever the sitter, but few buyers are interested in other people's

Sir Edwin Landseer: *Extensive Highland Landscape*. Oil, 20·3 × 24·2 cm.

Landseer's small landscape sketches have all the technical perfection without the gruesomeness or the winsomeness of many of his finished works.

ancestors by less well-known hands. I certainly would not advocate bulk-buying or anything like it in this field, but one good character study can add weight and distinction to a wall, and provide a centrepiece for paintings of other kinds.

John Frederick Herring, Senior: *Feeding the Horses.* Signed and dated 1854. Oil, 127 × 101·5 cm.

William F. Wilson: *A View of Quebec in Winter Looking across the St. Lawrence River, with Indians and Horses and Sleighs by a Quay.* Signed and dated Quebec 1851. Oil, 76·8 × 107·9 cm.

Because comparatively few artists worked in Canada, any early view, whether primitive or professional, is likely to be eagerly sought after.

Barend Cornelis Koekkoek: *A wooded winter landscape with a country house and farm cottages, numerous figures skating and conversing on a frozen river, and snow-covered fields in the distance.* Signed and dated 1839. Oil, 66 × 82·6 cm.

Another example of the technical ability but lack of originality of much mainstream nineteenth-century painting.

Jan Josefsz. van Goyen:
*A River Estuary with a
Customs House and a
Ferry nearby.* Signed
with initials and dated
1646. Oil,
37·5 × 53·3 cm.

(*Below*) Jean Bruegel the
Elder: *Allegory of Sight*.
1625. Oil, 64 × 108 cm.
Madrid, Prado.

Lucio Fontana: *Concetto Spaziale — Attesa*. Signed and inscribed with title on the reverse 'L. Fontana'. Oil, 46 × 38 cm.

The back of this painting is shown on page 27, and illustrates that the back can literally be more informative than the front.

The sale of Piet Mondrian's *Composition with Red, Blue and Yellow* at Christie's in London on 27 June 1983. The work fetched £1,512,000 ($2,328,480), then a record auction price for a work by the artist and for any abstract work of art.

John Constable: *Study of Sea and Sky*
(detail). Oil on paper laid down on card,
14 × 19·5 cm.

A simple-seeming sketch can sometimes
be more exciting than a formal and
finished painting.

7. Old Master Drawings

The term 'Old Master' is maddeningly imprecise. It means different things to different people and in different countries. In France or America it is not uncommon to find Hogarth or Reynolds labelled as Old Masters, while in Britain the French eighteenth-century masters are often regarded in the same way. Drawings which are Old Master in feel, but by English artists up to say 1750, will usually be classed with watercolours in Britain and, more logically, with Old Masters abroad. For the purist, I suppose, the term would only cover artists working before about 1700.

None of this, of course, need worry the collector, since his concern is enjoyment rather than semantics. As always, buy what you like of whatever period, country or school. However, there is a rational difference between earlier and later drawings, which may be described as one of language. Early drawings by the Italian, German and French masters are rarely intended as works of art in their own right, however artistic they may be. They tend to be preliminary working studies made during the preparation of some larger project in oil-paint, fresco, tempera or whatever. Otherwise they are memoranda to which the artist could refer at a later date. This is what makes them different from, say, English eighteenth-century watercolours, which were intended to stand as finished works conveying a particular impression to an audience beyond the artist himself. To change the metaphor slightly, those are careful copperplate script to the shorthand of the earlier working drawings.

This explains why the majority of the first collectors of drawings were themselves painters. Since there were few opportunities for most of them to study many great paintings for themselves, a collection of drawings was the best way to understand the mental processes and techniques of their predecessors and their foreign contemporaries. Often collections or single examples passed from painter to painter, and this can sometimes be traced through their collectors' marks.

In England one of the first and greatest of these artist-collectors was Sir Peter Lely (1618–80), and many of his drawings were acquired by his assistant Prosper Henricus Lankrink (or Lancrinck) (1628–92). From him they may have gone to the Jonathan Richardsons, father (c. 1665–1745) and son (1694–1771), or to the portrait painter Thomas Hudson (1701–79),

Francesco de' Rossi, Il Salviati: *The Baptism*. Black chalk heightened with white on blue paper, 39·5 × 27·7 cm.

(*Above*) Baccio della Porta,
Fra Bartolommeo: *A Tuscan Hill Town*.
Pen and brown ink, 20·5 × 27·7 cm.

Canaletto: *Two Seated Men, a Third
Standing*. Black ink, 9·2 × 13·3 cm.
London, National Gallery.

Raphael: *St. John and Two Apostles* and *Five Apostles*, studies for the *Charge to St. Peter.* c.1514–16. Red chalk over stylus indications, 8·4 × 11·6 cm. and 6·7 × 11·6 cm.

and thus to his pupil Sir Joshua Reynolds (1723–92). Paul Sandby (1725–1809) also accumulated a number of them, and in his turn Sir Thomas Lawrence (1769–1830) acquired drawings which had been owned by Sandby and Reynolds. By that time, of course, travel was easier, and it was no longer essential for artists to study drawings; but many painters did and do still collect them.

A good provenance of this sort can add considerably to the value (and the price) of a drawing, and any sensible collector will try to learn something of the tastes, strengths and weaknesses of his predecessors in the field. The practice of marking the drawings in a collection, either by

Canaletto: *The Piazzetta with the Torre dell'Orologio*. Pen and ink, 23·4 × 18 cm. Windsor, Royal Collection. Reproduced by gracious permission of H.M. Queen Elizabeth II.

Here the artist really is using shorthand – the figures in the foreground are given no more than one or two wiggly strokes. At the same time the view is immediately recognizable.

Io Zuane Antonio da Canal, deto il Canaleto lò Dissegnià è fatto.

fatta in Padoua e fata

Canaletto: *Padua: Houses*. Pen and brown/black ink, with grey wash. 22·8 × 15·8 cm. (overall). Kupferstichkabinett, Staatliche Museen Preussischer Kulturbesitz, Berlin (West).

The artist now in a more formal vein, producing a study for a title page.

hand or with a stamp, began early on and still continues. Such marks are usually placed discreetly at the edge or on the reverse of a drawing, but some people showed surprising insensitivity and arrogance by stamping within the actual composition. The formidable task of recording such marks and providing as much information about their users as possible was undertaken in the first half of this century by Fritz Lugt, resulting in his massive *Les Marques de Collections de Dessins et d'Estampes* (1921 and 1956). It is a work to which every collector must have access, even if he does not own it.

Drawings come in many different forms and are created from many different materials. Recently I saw an impressive nineteenth-century example which had been made at a dinner table using coffee and sealing

Bolognese School, seventeenth century: *Rinaldo and Armida*. Pen and brown ink, 20·7 × 15·7 cm.

Note the collectors' marks of Prosper Henry Lankrink and Peter Lely.

Sir Peter Lely: *Portrait of a Girl, probably Elizabeth Seymour, Countess of Ailesbury*. Signed. Black, red and white chalk on grey-brown paper, 28·3 × 19·7 cm.

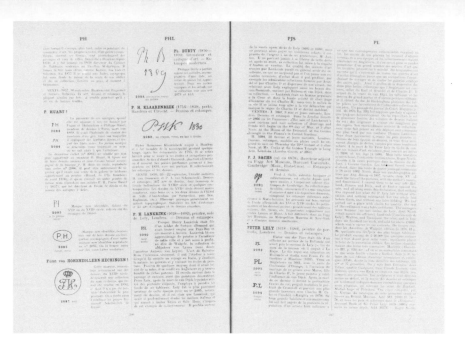

A page from Lugt showing Lankrink's and Lely's collectors' marks.

wax. Until the end of the eighteenth century artists generally made up their own pigments and inks, and almost anything might be pressed into service. The most common media for Old Master drawings are various forms of chalk and ink and wash. Old ink usually fades to brown, and it might be applied with a pen made from a quill or a reed, or laid in with a brush. Chalk is usually black or red, and the latter is known as sanguine when it has been mixed with iron oxide.

The favourite washes were brown and grey, although pink and blue are not uncommon. 'Grisaille' is used of a work in grey bodycolour, which unlike a wash is opaque. Sometimes touches of white bodycolour, or gouache, would be added, and these may have oxidized to an unsightly black. If you see a drawing where this has happened, it is worth consulting a restorer, since many of them can be recovered.

'Pencil' is a slightly ambiguous term. Originally it was used of any small brush used by an artist, and only gradually was it limited to the modern lead pencil, which, of course, is no longer made from lead, although its predecessors were. Other soft metals were also used, notably silver, which explains 'silverpoint' drawings. Charcoal has also always been used by artists, but early examples are rare since it is fugitive.

In many cases several different media will have been used in one drawing, and some catalogues try to give their descriptions in the order of application, as: 'black chalk, pen and brown ink and brown and grey wash heightened with white.'

You will sometimes find a drawing that has been 'squared', that is, covered in a grid of pencil or chalk. This will often indicate that a print has been made from it, or that the artist used it as a basis for some larger scheme such as a full painting or a mural. This should make your researches easier. On the other hand a drawing on prepared paper, that is, a sheet that has been stained or otherwise coloured before the drawing was made, may indicate that it was intended as a finished object in itself, rather than a working drawing, since good paper was too expensive to be used indiscriminately.

There are no hard and fast rules which dictate that certain subjects are best treated in certain media; that is something for the artist himself to decide. The eighteenth-century 'capriccio', for instance, a flight of fancy often based on classical buildings and ruins, is often particularly effective in brown wash, which conveys atmosphere so well, but red chalk can also achieve very good results. Italian exponents of the genre seem to have favoured the former, while Frenchmen such as Hubert Robert (1733–1808) chose the latter.

The nature of Old Master drawings is such that the collector must be something of a scholar and an art historian as well as the possessor of a good eye and feel. So often a little scrap in chalk or pen and ink will relate to a major painting or decorative scheme, and it is the job of the collector to know or discover which. If you have an aptitude for such work, it can be not only pleasurable, but ultimately very rewarding. The relationship of drawings and paintings also often makes possible more precise attribution than might seem possible at first glance, but to obtain such hard evidence you will need to learn about the history of painting as well as of drawing. Of course, the work will often have been done already by a dealer, auction house or earlier collector, but there are still plenty of opportunities of carving yourself a little niche in the form of a learned article on your researches in *The Burlington Magazine*.

Master of Flémalle (Robert Campin): *St. James the Greater and St. Clare*, from *The Betrothal of the Virgin*. Grisaille, 76·5 × 87 cm. Madrid, Prado.

An example of true 'grisaille' – albeit from a painting rather than a drawing – in which the image is made to look like sculpted stone by using only greys and white.

Sebastiano del Piombo: *A Prophet Addressed by an Angel*. Black chalk, slate-grey and brown wash heightened with on blue paper, squared in red chalk, 31·8 × 25·1 cm.

A study – almost a *grisaille* – for the mural in the Church of S. Pietro in Montorio, Rome, commissioned in 1516.

Albrecht Dürer: *Lucas van Leyden*. 1521. Silverpoint, 24·4 × 17·1 cm. Lille, Musée des Beaux-Arts.

This emphasis on the need for scholarship must not blind us to the aesthetic pleasures to be gained from early drawings, many of which are very decorative as well as of great academic interest. Obviously proof that a previously unattributed drawing is by Raphael or Michelangelo will greatly affect its price, but in many lesser cases an exact attribution does not greatly matter from the financial point of view, although it does of course from the point of view of scholarly satisfaction.

It is a big generalization to make, but in dealing with Old Master drawings you are unlikely to be greatly troubled by deliberate fakes. You may come across legitimate copies by contemporaries and later painters, but these have an interest and a value of their own. You must, however, always be on your guard against much later reproductions, whether photographic or otherwise, since these have abounded since the nineteenth century, and when seen through a glass dustily may just deceive. In the chapter on prints I mention what are known *as contre-épreuves*, which are reverse images made by laying a piece of paper on a print when the ink is still wet. These can also be taken from chalk drawings by wetting both papers. The impression is usually weaker than in the original, and the composition, being reversed, may look rather awkward. They will obviously have both a value and a price (since they are likely to have been made by the artist himself), but a lesser one than the original.

Rembrandt Harmensz. van Rijn: Studies of the head of a man for the Mauritshuis *Susannah and the Elders*. 1637. Pen and brown ink, cut lower left. 8·2 × 7·8 cm.

Hubert Robert: *Capriccio of Roman Ruins*. Red chalk and watercolour, 29·8 × 37·7 cm.

Raphael: *The Three Graces*.
*c.*1518. Red chalk over stylus,
20·3 × 26 cm. Windsor, Royal
Collection. Reproduced by
gracious permission of H.M.
Queen Elizabeth II.

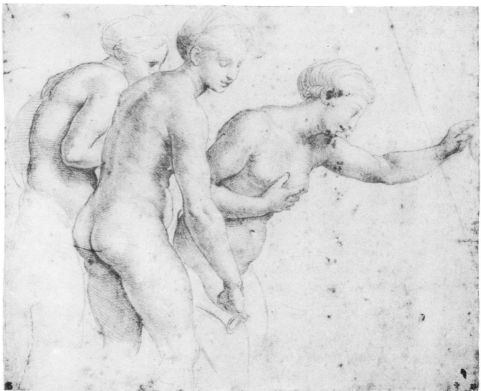

Raphael: *The Three Graces*
(counterproof). *c.*1518. Red
chalk, 22·6 × 27 cm. Chatsworth
House, Derbyshire.

Canaletto: Capriccio: *A Classic Triumphal Arch by the Lagoon*. Pen and ink, 19·4 × 27·1 cm. Windsor, Royal Collection. Reproduced by gracious permission of H.M. Queen Elizabeth II.

There is one group of modern forgeries, however, which beginners should watch out for. When the drawings appear in sale rooms that have recognized them, they are usually offered as 'Italian School' without any date. This is reasonable enough, since the forger seems to have worked in Italy, although he had, or has, English connections. They are pen-and-wash drawings and purport to be capricci in the manner of Canaletto or Francesco Guardi (1712–93). The brown or reddish ink has a dried-out appearance, as if it had been blotted immediately. This gives them a rather sickly feel which is quite easy to recognize with experience.

It has already been said that you should not automatically believe anything that you are told. The same is true of inscriptions on Old Master drawings. Many of them are mere guesses by older collectors. Others can be very helpful, pointing the way, perhaps through an old spelling, to an attribution, or to a subject and painting. As with anything else, always remember to look at the back of a drawing, and its frame if it has one.

The older the drawing, the less you will have to concern yourself with condition, by contrast with other fields of collecting. If, by immense good fortune, you were to obtain a perfect and highly finished cartoon by Raphael or Leonardo, then its value (and, once again, price) would be incalculable. It is more likely, although still improbable, that you would be dealing with a scrap, scarcely more than a doodle, which would be of an eccentric shape because cut from a larger sheet. It might well have been battered and stained and attacked by worms over the centuries, but no matter, it will have the touch of genius. It is up to you to see that it does not suffer still more while you are its temporary custodian.

8. Notes on Papermaking

Although Britain came late to papermaking in European terms, it is probably true to say that Britain led the world for a while in the technological advances of the mid-eighteenth century. The greatest change came in 1756, when the elder James Whatman pioneered 'wove' rather than 'laid' paper, although his products in this line did not become current until the 1770s. Paper was made from rags of cloth which were soaked and melded in sieve-like frames known as moulds. Originally the base of these would be made of parallel wires, which would leave a pattern of watermark lines in the paper. Whatman introduced a wire mesh, which gave greater support and therefore less obvious lines and a smoother surface.

Another Whatman invention was the 'Contrivance', a system of frames and pulleys which made it possible to produce larger sheets than before. (Size had hitherto been determined by the arm-span of the vatman.) This technique was perfected in 1772, and any sheet of paper which measures more than 53×31 in. (135×79 cm.) cannot have been produced before that date.

Although excise duty was charged on paper in Britain from 1712, mill numbers only appear in paper from the early nineteenth century until 1851. In a similar way dates were only necessary for tax purposes from 1794 to 1811, although many mills have continued to use them. A paper that has the mark 'J. Whatman Turkey Mill' in it almost certainly dates from after the sale of the business by the younger James Whatman in 1794, since the name had become synonymous with quality, and it is still in use today to indicate a standard.

Before the beginning of the nineteenth century, paper looked rough and hand-made. Thereafter it became smoother and was often rejected by artists. Science was not always the ally of art, and indeed the invention and introduction of bleach in the 1790s actually destroyed many watercolours because the acid used to make the paper white continued to work on the pigments. Blues were the most vulnerable, and they have often turned to pink where they have survived at all. This problem persisted after the introduction of wood-pulp and esparto grass as the raw materials for papermaking in the second half of the nineteenth century, and many artists sought out hand-made papers of older, vintage, years, as indeed they do today.

A further note worth remembering is that early home-made English tracing-paper often turned yellow, presumably because of the type of oil applied to the paper, whereas continental European examples have usually survived in better condition.

The earliest paper mill in America was established near Philadelphia in 1690. Mills opened in New Jersey and Massachusetts in the first third of the eighteenth century and in other places in the colonies in the decades following. A great deal of paper was, however, imported from England before the American Revolution, partly because tax-stamped paper had to be used for many legal purposes.

Much early American paper is watermarked and dated, but little study has been done of the history of American watermarks in comparison with European.

(*Left and above*) Stages in the making of paper by hand. The methods have changed little since the eighteenth century.

9. Caring for a Collection

Most people who buy watercolours are sensitive enough to know that they should not hang their purchases in direct sunlight. Not everybody will realize that light (whether natural or artificial), temperature and humidity can affect any sort of painting or print. People who have bought an oil painting do not always realize that they too should treat it with consideration.

Direct light, especially sunlight, will not just fade watercolours and affect any work on paper, but it can also damage the pigments of oil paintings. Humidity will rot canvas as well as paper. If you had just become a parent for the first time, you would realize that you had a responsibility to something fragile and helpless. A painting may not have the voice to complain, but it can be mistreated in the same way – unintentionally. The main theme of this book has been that you should be clear eyed when buying a picture; once you have bought one you have a responsibility to keep it in perfect condition just as if it were a child. Both a child and a good picture should outlast your lifetime.

People are often blissfully unaware of the damage that they are doing to their own possessions, and just fail to notice as they deteriorate. In the same way all too few people could actually describe their greatest treasure in an accurate way when it is not actually in front of them. Try, for a moment, and without looking at it, to describe your favourite painting so as to make it recognizable to a policeman or even a dealer. Do not wait until you are burgled before making a good catalogue of your collection, or having it professionally described and valued.

Prices and even values, can change very rapidly, and you should consider having your collection looked at by an expert at regular intervals. If you do not wish to go to this expense, then make your own catalogue, taking one of the better sale rooms or dealers as your model, and where possible take photographs. Even an instant print may be of help, although if you are a passable draughtsman, a line sketch of the main features can sometimes give a better impression. You must obviously keep

(*Opposite, below*) Frederic Whiting, *Self-portrait of the Artist*. c.1935. Oil, 88·9 × 73·7 cm. Private Collection.

On the left, the painting before cleaning; on the right, after the removal of nearly 50 years' grime.

Helen Bradley: *Oh, Cried Everyone as Father and Mr Taylor Carried the Picture*. Oil, 45·7 × 61 cm.

any such list, and even more so an insurance valuation, in a safe and preferably fire-proof place. It is not, after all, a bill of fare.

If after a time you should decide that you no longer enjoy something – or your whole collection – as much as you did, then sell it and let someone else enjoy it. If you are so minded you can start again. Always remember that the point of the whole business is enjoyment.

10. Further Reading

I wish that I were able to begin a bibliography on pictures with the splendid confidence of Robin Lane Fox in his biography of Alexander the Great: '1,472 books and articles are known to me on the subject [written] in the past century and a half', but our subject is too vast and too diverse for even the most well-fed computer to hazard more than a guess as to numbers of publications over that and previous periods. Some, however, should not be missed.

Works of Reference

There are a number of invaluable books to which a serious collector must know that he has easy access, even if he has neither the space nor the inclination to own them for himself. The most obvious of these are E. BÉNÉZIT, *Dictionnaire . . . des Peintres, Sculpteurs . . .* (10 vols., Paris, 1976) and the German equivalent, U. THIEME and F. BECKER, *Allgemeines Lexikon der Bildenden Kunstler* (37 vols., Leipzig, 1907–50), a splendid monument to German thoroughness. Naturally enough these two great works have a good deal in common, but equally naturally, each is particularly informative on the artists of its own country. Never forget that the dictionaries of national biography of your own and other countries can provide a great deal of information not only about painters, but also about sitters, subjects, houses and connections. The British *Dictionary of National Biography* (22 vols. and supplements, 1908–   ) gives lists and locations of portraits so far as they were known at the time of writing.

The collector of modern works should consult the *Phaidon Dictionary of 20th Century Art* (1971), and have library access to some such publication as the *International Directory of Arts* (2 vols., Frankfurt, 1979–80), which lists contemporary artists and also museums, valuers, restorers and so forth. Do not automatically dismiss seemingly outdated dictionaries and directories if you are dealing with older artists. Even something as venerable as M. BRYAN, *Dictionary of Painters and Engravers* (5 vols., 1926–34) can still yield the occasional nugget that has been overlooked by subsequent miners.

A good gazetteer can be a very useful tool, and in many cases an old one is actually more valuable than a modern, since it (and you) will not be confused by twentieth-century changes and developments. In this library section remember F. LUGT, *Les Marques de Collections de Dessins et d'Estampes* (1921, 1956), and W. A. CHURCHILL, *Watermarks in Paper* (1935).

Biographical dictionaries of artists such as Bénézit and Thieme and Becker, cited above, are generally weak on American artists. There are two standard works in print that are invaluable for research on American artists: GEORGE C. GROCE and DAVID H. WALLACE, *The New-York Historical Society Dictionary of Artists in America, 1564–1860* (New Haven, Yale University Press, 1957) and MANTLE FIELDING, *Dictionary of American Painters, Sculptors and Engravers* (many editions, of which the best is New York, James F. Carr, 1965, since it updates many of the entries and has a large addendum of new material).

The most important American exhibition records that have been published are: MARIA NAYLOR, *The National Academy of Design Exhibition Record, 1861–1900*, (2 vols., New York, Kennedy Galleries, Inc., 1973); ANNA WELLS RUTLEDGE, *The Pennsylvania Academy of the Fine Arts, 1807–1870, Record of Exhibition Catalogues* (Philadelphia, American Philosophical Society, 1955); and ROBERT F. PERKINS, JR. and WILLIAM J. GAVIN III, *The Boston Athenaeum Art Exhibition Index, 1827–1874* (Boston, Athenaeum, 1980); and CLARK S. MARLOR, *A History of the Brooklyn Art Association* (New York, James F. Carr, 1970).

Schools of Artists

Over the last couple of decades biographical dictionaries devoted to local and national schools and types of painting have blossomed in many countries. I remember being rather dismissive of G. SCHURR, *Les Petits Maîtres de la Peinture Valeur de Demain* in a review when the first volume appeared in 1972, but I have subsequently found it and its sequels very useful. Britain is well catered for in the publications of the Antique Collectors' Club, notably E. H. H. ARCHIBALD, *Dictionary of Sea Painters* (1980); H. L. MALLALIEU, *Dictionary of British Watercolour Artists up to 1920* (1976, 1979); E. WATERHOUSE, *Dictionary of British 18th Century Painters* (1981); and C. WOOD, *Dictionary of Victorian Painters* (1978).

From other publishers Ireland is well served by ANNE CROOKSHANK and the KNIGHT OF GLIN in *The Painters of Ireland* (1978), which should be taken in conjunction with W. G. STRICKLAND, *A Dictionary of Irish Artists* (1913, repr. 1965), and Scotland by D. and F. IRWIN, *Scottish Painters at Home and Abroad* (1975), which goes hand in hand with the joyous J. CAW, *Scottish Painting* (1908, repr. 1975).

Among books on special areas or periods of American art of use to collectors may be mentioned: PAUL CUMMINGS, *A Dictionary of Contemporary American Artists* (New York, St. Martin's Press, 1966); PEGGY and HAROLD SAMUELS, *The Illustrated Biographical Encyclopedia of Artists of the American West* (Garden City, Doubleday, 1976); and JIM COLLINS and GLENN B. OPITZ, *Women Artists in America* (Poughkeepsie, N.Y., 1980).

On the whole the beginner should be wary of bare listings, such as the publications of Algernon Graves on Royal Academy exhibitors, or price guides and lists, since they can mislead by the very paucity of information. They are aids which are best left to the professional.

Auctions and Dealers

This is another area which has produced a growing volume of literature in recent years. In no particular order I would mention the following: D. and K. LEAB, *The Auction Companion* (1981); J. COOPER, *Under the Hammer* (1977); R. WRAIGHT, *The Art Game Again* (1974), which is a rewriting and updating of *The Art Game* (1965); F. HERMANN, *Sotheby's: Portrait of an Auction House* (1980); P. COLSON, *A Story of Christie's* (1950); D. SUTTON, *Christie's since the War* (1959); W. TOWNER, *The Elegant Auctioneers* (1971), which deals with Parke Bernet; S. N. BEHRMAN, *Duveen* (1973), an inspiration to anyone who might consider becoming a dealer; J. RUSSELL TAYLOR and J. BROOKE, *The Art Dealers* (1969); R. GIMPEL, *Diary of a Picture Dealer* (1966).

Forgeries

Every ten years or so a book such as S. SCHÜLLER, *Forgers, Dealers, Experts* (1959, Eng. trans. 1960) appears dealing with fakes and forgeries. There is not a great deal to choose between them, but any serious collector should read one of them, preferably whichever is the most recent, since it will have added a few new anecdotes and case histories to the usual stock.

Prints

The *Burlington* is of great use here, too, as also are the bi-monthly *Print Collector's Newsletter* in the United States, and the many volumes of the *Print Collector's Quarterly*, which should be found in any good art reference library. The *Print Collector's Newsletter* began bi-monthly publication in New York in 1970. It provides ample information on the print world: exhibitions, catalogues, new editions of prints and portfolios, auction prices, and lists of dealers and their publications, as well as general articles on the collecting of both Old Master and Modern prints in the U.S. and abroad. The back issues of the *Print Collector's Quarterly*, published in New York and elsewhere between 1911 and 1951 contain many valuable articles on prints and printmakers that are still useful.

An important market publication is *Gordon's Print Price Annual* (New York, Martin Gordon, Inc., 1978–) which covers in great depth print auction results in both the U.S. and abroad.

There are many specialist tomes on the individual methods or printmaking: a good place to start is *How Prints Look* (New York, Metropolitan Museum of Art, 1943 and later reprints), a paperback book by WILLIAM IVINS, a former curator at the Metropolitan. A fairly extensive bibliography will be found in A. BUCHSBAUM, *A Practical Guide to Print Collecting* (1975).

Classic works which should still find a place on the shelf include A. M. HIND, *A History of Engraving and Etching* (1923, repr. 1963), and J. H. SLATER, *Engravings and their Value* (repr. 1978). An enthusiast of sporting prints should spend as long as it takes in second-hand bookshops to run down F. SILTZER, *The Story of British Sporting Prints* (1929), since its rambling charm could almost turn a hunt saboteur into a follower. Anyone with an interest in fine twentieth-century etching and who is also a lover of beautiful books and has a long pocket should seek out K. GUICHARD, *British Etchers 1850–1940* (1977), making sure that it contains the original prints by Robin Tanner. This also gives details of Australian etchers.

In doing research on American prints the following works are indispensable: JOHN D. MORSE, ed., *Prints in and of America to 1850* (Winterthur, Delaware, Henry Francis du Pont Museum, 1970); FRANK WEITENKAMPF, *American Graphic Art* (most recent edition New York, Johnson, 1970); DAVID MCNEELY STAUFFER, *American Engravers upon Copper and Steel*, 2 vols. (New York, Grolier Club, 1907 and reprints). For collectors of American lithographs the two monumental works by HARRY T. PETERS, *America on Stone* (New York, Doubleday, 1931) and *Currier & Ives: Printmakers to the American People*, 2 vols. (New York, Doubleday, 1929–31) are indispensable.

Watercolours

No collector should be without the trinity, J. L. ROGET, *History of the Old Water Colour Society* (repr. 1972); I. O. WILLIAMS, *Early English Watercolours* (repr. 1971); and at least the third volume of M. HARDIE, *Watercolour Painting in Britain* (1967–9). There are many general surveys of the subject. I would perhaps recommend LAURENCE BINYON, *English Water-Colours* (repr. of 2nd edn. 1962). Binyon, surprisingly, was never a collector, but he was a poet and that informs his eye and prose. Also greatly to be recommended is H. LEMAÎTRE, *Le Paysage Anglais à l'Aquarelle* (1955). On specific areas, especially Turner, the writings of ANDREW WILTON and his collaborators MARTIN BUTLIN and EVELYN JOLL are authoritative. For the social and scientific background there are M. CLARKE, *The Pleasing Prospect* (1981); and H. L. MALLALIEU, *Understanding English Watercolours* (1984). K. ETHERIDGE, *Collecting Drawings* (1970) deals with watercolours for the most part, and is good on the market.

Old Master Drawings

The bulk of the essential literature will be found in the form of articles in the more scholarly magazines, such as *The Burlington Magazine, Old Master Drawings, Connaissance des Arts* and *Weltkunst*.

Paper

The doyen of the historians of paper was DARD HUNTER, and his *Papermaking* (1967) contains the bulk of what it is necessary for the collector to know, although more recent research has added to it. The standard book on American antique paper is DARD HUNTER, *Papermaking by Hand in America* (Chillicothe, Ohio, Mountain House Press, 1950).

Restoration

For those who might wish to chance their arms at restoration, H. PLENDERLEITH, *The Conservation of Antiquities and Works of Art* (1957) contains a section on prints and drawings. I hope, though, that it will persuade most people to turn to a professional.

Almost any bookshop in the world, whether new or second-hand, will have something that will be relevant to your concerns. A further joy of picture collecting is that one becomes, almost without noticing, a collector of books as well. It might help to begin by consulting L. LUCAS, *Art Books: A Basic Bibliography on the Fine Arts* (1968), which lists more than 6,000 titles and comes in paperback.

Appendix

Much of the information that the picture buyer will need is most sensibly obtained by word of mouth. Personal recommendation is the best advertisement when looking for a dealer, sale room, restorer or other expert. However there are a number of publications which can provide a starting point.

In the U.S. there is *The International Art Market* (Box 75, Woodbury, New York, 11797) and *The Artnewsletter* (published by *Artnews Magazine*, 5 West 37th Street, New York, N.Y. 10018).

One of the most comprehensive surveys of the field is the *International Directory of Arts* published annually by Art Address Verlag, Munich, and by Bowker and Company, New York. Among other subjects this covers, country by country, museums, associations, dealers, auctioneers, restorers, publishers and periodicals.

For the sale rooms of the world there is *The Auction Companion* by D. and K. Leab (London, 1981), and other stand-bys are the biennial *Guide Emer* (Paris), which covers much of Europe as well as France, and *The International Art and Antiques Yearbook* (London). Naturally there are also national directories of dealers and of the art world such as *The British Art and Antiques Yearbook* (London), and *The American Art Directory* (New York, published triennially).

For a detailed coverage of the market there is the weekly newspaper *The Antiques Trade Gazette* (Langley House, 116 Long Acre, London WC2). Its listings of forthcoming sales and reports of recent ones, together with exhibitions, advertisements and trade news, cover the international art and antiques market, not just the British. It is a tool for the professional, and is most easily obtained by annual subscription.

The needs of the beginner are expressly catered for in the *Christie's Guide to Collecting* edited by Robert Cumming (Oxford, 1984), which gives practical advice on all aspects of collecting, including buying and selling, insurance, shipping, restoration and taxation.

There are many lists and guides to museums, both on the national and on the international level, the most detailed being *The Directory of Museums* (London, 1975), which appeared in the United States as *The Directory of World Museums* (Columbia University Press, 1974).

Two professional bodies in Britain may be of use to the buyer, especially if he has complaints to make. For dealers there is the Society of London Art Dealers (c/o The Fine Art Society, 148 New Bond Street, London W1Y 0JT) and for sale rooms the Society of Fine Art Auctioneers (7 Blenheim Street, New Bond Street, London W1Y 0AS). Neither Christie's nor Sotheby's are members of the latter. Remember, too, that many members of the British Antique Dealers' Association (20 Rutland Gate, London SW7 1BD) and the London and Provincial Antique Dealers' Association (112 Brompton Road, London SW3 1JJ) will handle paintings from time to time, and that membership implies both quality and a high standard of professional ethics.

Any specialist dealer or auctioneer in Britain should be able to provide you with a valuation for insurance or probate purposes. Many of the larger estate agents also have a chattels division which can provide the same services.

In the United States those needing valuations could turn to the American Society of Appraisers (P.O. Box 17265, Washington DC 20041), to the Appraisers Association of America (60 East 42 Street, New York, NY 10165), or to the International Society of Appraisers (P.O. Box 726, Hoffman Estates, Illinois 60195). Each publishes a directory of members and their specialities.

North American dealers' groups include the Art and Antique Dealers' League of America (353 East 53 Street, New York, NY 10022), the Art Dealers' Association of America (575 Madison Avenue, New York NY 10022) and the National Antique and Art Dealers' Association of America (15 East 57 Street, New York NY 10022).

Index

Numbers in italic refer to pages on which illustrations occur.

CREDITS

The majority of the illustrations in this book are reproduced from photographs from the archives of Christie's and Phaidon Press. Acknowledgement is also due to the following: